TOWPATHS
OF
ENGLAND

The tunnel under the road at Posset Bridge, Marple, on the Peak Forest Canal.

Towpaths
of
England

Brian Bearshaw

Line illustrations
by David Chesworth

A COMET BOOK

A Comet Book
Published in 1986
by the Paperback Division of
W.H. Allen & Co. PLC
44 Hill Street, London W1X 8LB

First published in Great Britain by Robert Hale Ltd

Copyright © Brian Bearshaw 1985

Printed and bound in Great Britain by
Biddles Ltd, Guildford and King's Lynn

ISBN 0 86379 099 2

Contents

By the same author

Lancashire Cricket at the Top (joint editor)
Waterside Walks in Lancashire

Fiction
The Day of Murder
Practice Makes Murder
The Order of Death

List of Illustrations

Drawn by David Chesworth

To Mum

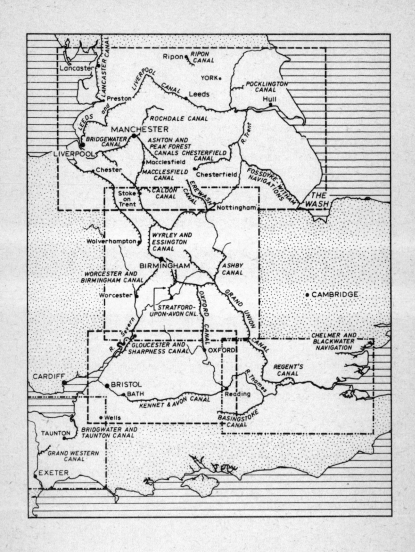

Preface

The canals of England have changed in two hundred years from prosperous commercial highways to sleepy lanes for pleasure boats, angling and walking. Working boats have almost vanished from the waterways, most of which are now peaceful backwaters, abounding in wild life and plant life, running for miles through the heart of the countryside. They make easy, relaxed walking, they are flat and usually quiet, they do not run through anybody's land, disturbing livestock or flattening crops, and it is almost impossible to get lost on a canal bank. There are the occasional hills, of course, at locks and over tunnels, some of them quite long and impressive like the flights of locks at Caen Hill on the Kennet and Avon, at Wigan on the Leeds and Liverpool, Marple on the Peak Forest, and Tardebigge on the Worcester and Birmingham. It is possible to walk miles without seeing a person, with only the moorhens and squirrels for company, with buildings no more obtrusive than scattered farms. I saw herons on nearly every canal; I watched a water vole having its lunch on a plank in the Basingstoke, and thrilled at the sight of kingfishers all over the country, including four on the Leeds and Liverpool Canal.

So much of the industry that made the canals has gone. But many reminders remain, reminders of two hundred years in which the Industrial Revolution swept across the land. For me, however, it was the peace, the isolation, that made it so enjoyable in so many different parts of England. Not another soul. Just the countryside, the beautiful English countryside. And even in industrial centres the canals could weave their way quietly through, behind hedges and banks and walls, almost unnoticed now the working boats have gone.

The canals in this book were a purely personal choice, mostly taken at random but covering as many different parts of England as I could. I have tried hard to eliminate error, and to those members of various canal societies who have helped and made suggestions, I am grateful.

London
and its Surrounding
Areas

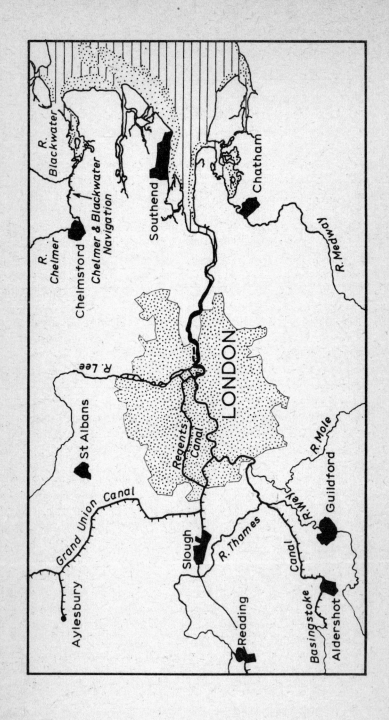

1

Regent's Canal

The Regent's Canal is something special. Simply because it is in London. It runs from Paddington to the Thames, from the elegant surroundings of Little Venice to the East End dockland at Limehouse. It goes over a lot of familiar ground: Maida Vale and Edgware Road, Regent's Park, Primrose Hill and Camden Town, King's Cross, St Pancras, Islington, Hackney, Bethnal Green and Stepney. Lord's cricket ground is just up the road as the canal crosses Lisson Grove, Regent's Park Zoo is sliced by it, Chapel Market sits on top of it. All London is here. Its sights, sounds, smells, its very heart and soul. It passes within sniffing distance of a Robert Carrier restaurant, it carries a cruising restaurant, but I suspect it feels more at home with the pie and mash and jellied eels of its East End caffs. It puts on its finery in Regent's Park and Little Venice but looks more itself when it rolls up its sleeves with the working people.

The old Chapel Market in Islington, a genuine market with real prices, typifies the canal and its people. The canal runs underground for half a mile to get through Islington, part of it directly beneath Chapel Street, whose householders protested when the tunnel was dug in 1820. There is a warmth and honesty about your real East End market. The hard sell is friendly. 'Lovely peaches, guv.' A barrow girl puts a few good-looking cabbages to the front. 'How are you, luv?' Men in braces and flat caps shoulder through with boxes of crisp lettuces and shiny red apples. ''Ere we are, mi old cock sparrow, only 10p a pound.' Women, fat and cheery with beefy arms and rosy faces, bustle about, serving, weighing, counting, wrapping, tearing down paper bags, digging deep in their apron pockets for change. From a nearby pub comes the thumping sound of the old joanna, pumped out by a bright-eyed bloke who has spent his life making his music heard above the hubbub.

It is all rather different four miles away, a shade more genteel with some fine Georgian houses accompanying the canal along its closing stages to the delightful junction at Little Venice where the Regent's meets the Paddington arm and runs into the Grand Union Canal to Brentford and the Midlands. I approached Little Venice from Marble Arch, up Edgware Road, along Harrow Road and off through Paddington Green, the old village centre. Gravestones lined the wall: 'To the memory of Mary Thrupp, an affectionate wife, a tender parent, or to sum up all in one, a Real Christian, died 1795 aged 38.' Then Little Venice, watched over by Warwick Crescent and Maida Avenue, a watery triangle with its island of weeping willows, blessed by a beautiful background of blossom, wide, tree-lined avenues, Georgian houses. I sat for a time soaking up a scene that could have changed little from the time of Robert Browning, who lived in Warwick Crescent in the last century. I was on a bench with a name: 'The Maisie Seat. May all who use and care for it have good health, good fortune and happiness.'

The canal has hardly got underway when it plunges into its other tunnel, 272 yards through Maida Hill. I crossed Edgware Road and went up Aberdeen Place to the Crown, a real ale pub which is a popular watering hole from Lord's, close by on St John's Wood Road. As the road turns left, a footpath on the other side leads down steps to the canal, the path going through a short tunnel and up a steep, curving path, the way the horses used to go. A shower kept me under the railway bridge with the cooing pigeons before I was able to go into Regent's Park, once a royal hunting ground for Henry VIII, then laid out by John Nash about the time the canal was being constructed, both being named after the Prince Regent, later George IV.

The Hanoverians, of course, had to be commemorated, and to the right as the canal enters the park is Hanover Gate, Terrace and Mews. The Terrace, built in 1822, housed H. G. Wells, the novelist, at No. 13, and Vaughan Williams, the composer, at No. 11. Charles Dickens wrote part of *Great Expectations* while staying at No. 3 in 1861. There is not much of the park to see from the canal which sneaks along the northern edge, deep in its cutting, between Prince Albert Road and the park's Outer Circle Road. Another shower, heavier and longer, kept me under the Macclesfield Bridge, one of the most talked-about features of the canal after a spectacular explosion there in 1874. The bridge, named after the canal company's first chairman, the Earl of

Macclesfield Bridge on the Regent's Canal, re-built after being accidentally blown up in 1874.

Macclesfield, also became known as 'Blow-up Bridge' after a barge called *Tilbury*, carrying forty barrels of gunpowder, exploded as it was being towed under it. Three crewmen were killed and nearby houses were damaged. As I paced about beneath the re-built bridge, watching the rain beating down on the water, I felt the tow-rope grooves – on the wrong side of the pillars! The bridge's ten iron supporting columns had survived the blast and had been replaced with the rope marks to the inside when it was re-built. A slit in a plane tree close by was also caused by the explosion. I wondered if the shock had stunted its growth as well. It did not look a hundred years old.

As I waited for the rain to go away, I watched a boat, with only four passengers and a driver done up in oilskins from head to toe, sail by on the way to Regent's Park Zoo, situated on both sides of the canal. The aviary designed by Lord Snowdon is right against the towpath, and I spent many unrewarding minutes peering through the shrubbery for those well-known birds, the Red-Billed Whistling Duck and the Greater Necklaced Laughing Thrush. Further along was the pheasantry, the owls' aviary and the paddock for cranes and geese.

A church bell ringing somewhere in Camden Town called me on. I left the whistling duck and laughing thrush and the other hysterical bird-life as I headed for Cumberland Basin, a mooring area where the canal once forked to continue round the park to the Cumberland Hay Market near Euston. In an article in *Harper's New Monthly Magazine* in 1885 the author wrote: 'The arm to the right turns south along the east edge of Regent's Park, among fine residences, past the great Albany cavalry barracks, for half a mile or so, ending in the Jew's harp basin. We kept on to the left among stately mansions.' And so did I, out of the park and alongside several grand Victorian houses which run down to the water with willow trees and rowing boats. A reminder of the more routine accidents that could occur on a canal comes with a plaque on the wall near a ramp in the water: 'The ramp up to the towpath opposite this wall is one of a pair either side of the railway bridge and was used to rescue horses which, when startled by the trains, sometimes bolted and fell into the canal.'

I try to walk the Regent's Canal at weekends so I can sample the excitements of another market at Camden Lock with its brass and noise and life. Here are the first of the twelve locks that carry the canal down to the Thames, an attractive area with a fine iron roving bridge with deep tow-rope grooves in the iron and stone, and the original 1815 lock cottage.

The elegance and nobility of the area around Regent's Park have given way to the working London. The East End is not all that far away. The Post Office tower with its head in the air appears above the buildings. Close behind comes the impressive sight of St Pancras railway station with its tall twin towers, viewed between a gathering of black gas holders. Euston and

King's Cross are over there as well, and an arm on the right for the London Narrow Boat Association has a wharf at the end with the sign 'Jams and Marmalade. Plaistowe and Co.'

It was time for Islington Tunnel. I could see clear through to light at the other end and could hear the chug of a boat going through. For over a hundred years boats were towed through by a steam tug which pulled itself along a chain on the canal bed. The *Harper's Magazine* article described the tunnel: 'Ahead of us rises a hill, at its feet the open mouth of Islington Tunnel, and we haul up alongside the towpath, and other barges and monkey boats come up and form a little fleet, all waiting for the tug that is to tow us through.' And then: 'It is five o'clock; out of the mouth of the tunnel come in dramatic procession two monkey-boats lashed together, like the catamarans of Brazil, pushed by the tug which tows in turn a long line of barges behind. It is a queer sort of boat – a very broad-bottomed barge, almost the width of the tunnel; from its flat deck rises an arched iron structure nearly filling the interior of the vault. The air we breathe is almost as poisonous as the delectable compound called by that name provided for the passengers by the underground railway.'

I followed the canal line over the hill as best I could, through the estate, Half Moon Crescent Housing Co-operative, past the unemployment benefit office and the White Conduit pub, across Barnsbury Road and through Chapel Market – 'Sorry, no eels today,' apologized a sign in a café window. I cannot say I was sorry. The last lot of eels I had made me feel sick. Upper Street and Islington High Street lie in front, a wide, imposing thoroughfare which carried the stage-coach to the far north. Islington Gate, with the turnpike and small toll house, once marked the end of urban London. Rural England lay ahead. The Angel, Islington, so familiar from the game of Monopoly, had great stables and ample accommodation. Islington, once popular for its waters, appealed to the writer Oliver Goldsmith two centuries ago: 'A pretty, neat town, mostly built of brick, with a church and bells; it has a small lake, or rather pond, in the midst, though at present very much neglected. I am told it is dry in summer.'

Across Islington High Street, past 'The York', down Duncan Street and back to the canal where *Olive*, a big old barge, watched over a scene of quiet elegance with more Georgian houses. In a minute or two I was at the City Road Basin, a branch that

brimmed with boats, hemmed in by office blocks and reminding
me of the skyline of Sydney or San Francisco. Well, almost . . .

Houses and flats were coming nearer. The sound of a brass
band blared across a deserted playground, and the smell of
dinner tantalizingly drifted past. A baby bawled, and a tired
mother bawled back. I was in Hackney, where yet another market
stood next to the canal – Broadway market, rundown and holding
on to the little life it has on Fridays and Saturdays.

The canal opens out into a pleasant tree-lined stretch at the start
of Victoria Park, one of the entrances to which is at Bonner Hall
Bridge, a rather nice piece of work with ironwork railings and the
initials V.R. on it. The Victoria, London's oldest municipal park
from the middle of last century, was at its brightest. At Old Ford
Lock people were strolling, sitting, fishing. There is a lake near
the towpath. After the Royal Cricketers pub, with a canalside
terrace, comes the Hertford Union canal, 1¼ miles long, straight
as a broom handle, a short cut to the River Lea near Hackney
Wick. A sunburnt man in shorts walked past, reading the *Hackney
Gazette* and accompanied by two spotty dogs. Two lovely, red
London buses, both No. 8s, went over the bridge carrying Roman
Road. There are pretty houses near the Mile End Road and a
sewer chimney at Tower Hamlets, shortly after which come
Salmon Lane Lock and the end of the towpath. A fence, barbed
wire and a 'Private. Keep Out. Beware of Dog' sign would be
more than enough for most people, but for those desperate to see it
through, like me, there was a break in the fence about 150 yards on.

The enormous Limehouse Basin and the Thames were only
minutes away. It was sad to see the Basin with its great lock gates
and its huge area of nothingness and neglect. Once it throbbed
with life. Daniel Defoe wrote in 1724: 'That part of the river
Thames which is properly the harbour and where the ships
usually deliver or unload their cargoes, is called the Pool, and
begins at the turning of the river out of Lime-house Reach, and
extends to the Custom-house Keys. In this compass I have had
the curiosity to count the ships as well as I could, and have found
above two thousand sail of all sorts, not reckoning barges,
lighters or pleasure boats, and yachts; but vessels that really go to
sea.'

And the *Harper's Magazine* 160 years later, on the Limehouse
Basin: 'On the quays and in the water is a busy scene. Men and

Camden Lock, with its machinery and bridge, on the Regent's Canal.

machinery are at work loading and unloading vessels of every build and every rig, lying alongside the jetties or in the basin, beleaguered by barges. There are sloops and schooners and brigs, paddle-wheel steamers and screw colliers, bluff bowed Dutch boats, sharp and shapely coasters, some low in the water with their heavy cargoes, some high out, already unladen.'

I sat and looked out over the vast emptiness, and dreamed.

DISTANCE OF WALK: 8½ MILES.   **OS MAP 1:25,000 series
TQ 28/38**

Grand Union Canal

The Grand Union Canal, composed of several separate canals, has a main line of 135 miles from the River Thames at Brentford to Birmingham. There are other arms and sections, building the entire Grand Union system up to more than three hundred miles. Here is a selection:

Three of the Midlands sections are discussed later on (p. 101) but here is the Brentford portion.

Brentford–Uxbridge–Paddington

I took the train to Brentford Central and walked to the High Street and along Dock Road to the great river of England, the Thames. I was right opposite Kew Gardens, and the temptation was strong to walk by the river downstream to the city or up to Richmond, Kingston and Hampton Court, my favourite summer walk when in London. I did neither. I turned my back on the river and gazed for a few minutes at the large tidal locks where the Grand Union starts its long journey north. It was a lovely, cloudless morning, fanned by a gentle breeze, as I wandered along to Syon Park on the Duke of Northumberland's estate. Samuel Pepys regularly visited Thomas Povy at his country house at 'Branford'.

The canal continues across Brentford High Street to Lock No. 100, a major trans-shipment centre for goods from the north when the first section of the canal, then the Grand Junction, was opened between Brentford and Uxbridge in 1794. The towpath runs on under the canopied warehouses, a cool relief from the hot sun but eerie, I should think, at the wrong time of day. A good introduction, a sort of aperitif, to the M4 motorway, comes with the Great West Road.

Coaches whizzed by on the motorway, a TWA jumbo jet lifted itself into the blue yonder, all far removed from the still of the canal. Just ahead is Gallows Bridge, a fine iron and latticed footbridge carrying the towpath to the opposite side: 'Horseley

Iron Works, near Birmingham, 1820.' Under the London Underground's Piccadilly Line, under the M4, through an area thick with elderberry, watching the swallows swooping and airliners sliding into Heathrow. A footbridge takes the path over the River Brent which has been canalized from Brentford. A patient from the neighbouring St Bernard's Hospital sat in a dressing-gown at the edge of the bottom lock on the Hanwell flight. The hospital had originally been called Hanwell Asylum, and one of the locks keeps the name alive with the title, Asylum Lock. Close by is the arch, now bricked up, that formed the entrance to the hospital's own dock. Beyond the top lock is Three Bridges, with the railway, canal and road together, leading into a pleasant stretch around Norwood Locks, which is riverlike with boats tucked in beneath the trees. A stone post declares the number of miles to the Thames; a lovely-sounding pub, the Old Oak Tree, is followed by a row of houses, 'Industrious Cottages'. There were a few house-boats for sale nearby, one offering a 'complete flat afloat – hall, lounge, beds, bathroom, kitchen – offers'. Had its own water lilies, too.

Bull's Bridge junction signposts the turn-off to Paddington, straight ahead for Birmingham with the sight and sound and smell of one of the first Nestlé chocolate factories built in this country. Not far past West Drayton railway station was the Slough Arm, constructed to serve the many brickfields in the area. Close by was the Packet Boat Dock, the terminus of the fifteen-mile Paddington–Cowley packet boat service which ran at the start of the nineteenth century but survived only five years. Nearly two hundred years ago – and there is still a Packet Boat Lane and a Paddington Packet Boat Inn.

I turned back at Uxbridge and returned to Bull's Bridge with its nineteenth-century canalside cottage and branch off to Little Venice at Paddington and into the Regent's Canal. This part of the canal was once thronged with arms and docks for brickfields and factories, even jam and biscuit manufacturers. Some large industry survives, like the Lyon's Tetley factory at Greenford, the Glaxo works and the Mother's Pride bakery. Horsenden Hill, Sudbury Golf Course and Perivale Wood provide a welcome rural setting, lovely walking right up to the cemetery at Wembley. An aqueduct carries the canal over the North Circular Road, not a particularly impressive sight but for once I was at least looking

Hanwell Lock cottage on the Grand Union Canal.

down on the traffic. The canal goes on past Harlesden and Willesden and the blur of railway lines, past Wormwood Scrubs with its prison and the open expanse where many attempts at flying were made by the pioneers early in the century. The canal touches the edge of two more cemeteries, one of them Kensal Green, first used in 1832 and which used to receive coffins from canal barges. Harrow Road comes in close as the canal moves into Paddington and the delightful area of Little Venice.

DISTANCE OF WALK: 31 MILES.   **OS MAP 176**

Basingstoke Canal

My first visit to the Basingstoke Canal was one of those spur-of-the-moment decisions. I was in London with two days to spare between cricket matches, and glorious weather persuaded me to take an early train to Fleet. I travelled light with just a toothbrush. Literally. And I had to find somewhere to stay for the night. I was on the canal towpath for ten o'clock and started by walking the beautiful ten miles to Greywell Tunnel. More walking through the lovely Hampshire lanes and a short train ride returned me to Fleet and the start of the amble towards the junction with the Wey Navigation at Woodham twenty-seven miles away. I thought I would find an inn for the night at Aldershot, a sizeable town with a population of 35,000, the home of the British Army. Somehow I managed to miss it and resigned myself to curling up under the hawthorns. After all, it had been a lovely, lovely day, and we were only four days from the longest day in the year. I was still thinking about it when I came to Ash, where the landlord at a nearby pub found me a room a mile away at the Chester Arms. I was glad. I had walked in light, soft-soled shoes, and my feet were sore. I was wakened once in the night. By the rain. I thought briefly of the hedge on the canal, smiled smugly and snuggled down. My second visit was the following summer, with fond memories of the delightful countryside, peaceful seclusion, the leafy, wooded tunnels I had enjoyed. I remembered particularly my first experience, from Fleet to Greywell.

The canal is beautiful at Fleet, with overhanging trees, heavy banks of rhododendrons, the flowers in full bloom. It did not look to have rained for weeks. The ground was dry, almost parched, and a dusty film had settled on the still water. Within minutes I had seen the flower I came to associate with the Basingstoke, the yellow iris, a bright and beautiful wild plant that was everywhere. The sun shone strongly from the duck-egg blue sky, but there was no way through for it on some of the stretches where trees gather like football crowds to bring welcome leafy shade to the path. Huge, old, powerful oak trees look to have been there hundreds of years, helping to intensify a silence broken only occasionally by the song of a bird or the hum of a bee or the drone of an aeroplane.

A class of young schoolchildren gathered at a swing bridge. 'Miss' pulled it with its chain to show how it worked, then started to tell the children about the natural life all around them. I asked about the underwater plant, reaching for air and moving as lithely as a ballet dancer. She told me it was called horsetail and was one of the oldest forms of aquatic life. I thanked her. She smiled and roared: 'Third form over here.' It was enough to send the moorhens splashing through the weeds, a wood pigeon flew off and a squirrel scuttled away before stopping to watch warily out of the corner of its eye.

Poulters Bridge – 'Built 1782. Restored 1977. Crookham Village Association' – leads the way into Crookham village and the Chequers Inn, haunted by the ghost of a man involved in a shotgun accident at the inn. Boatmen and their horses used to be boarded here, a contract with the canal company entitling the landlord to 5d – the present 2p – a night for each man. For this he got a straw bed in the stable loft, a clay pipe and tobacco. Horses cost rather more. They were stabled and fed for 9d.

It was around here that I had my first sight of the defence system built in 1940 in the event of an invasion by the Germans. I did not know what they were at first, large concrete slabs diagonally facing across the water and about a gate's width apart. I was just past the Blacksmith's Bridge when I found out. 'Tank-traps,' said a man with a bicycle and the *Daily Mirror*. 'Tank-traps. Waste of concrete. And see those bunkers?' He pointed to a pill-box, built into the ground, standing about four feet above it. 'They were manned in the war. It was very quiet here. They must have been bored out of their minds. All part of the invasion scare.' The line of defences ran from near Middlesbrough to the Wash and Cambridge, east of London and to Maidstone, and across southern England to Bristol. It was hoped to harass the enemy and protect London and industrial areas.

Another hour's walking through quiet country with little more than dragonflies – or were they damselflies? – and butterflies, one brilliantly blue, for company, brought me to Colt Hill Bridge. 'Rowing boats, punts and motor boats for hire here.' Greywell

One of the locks on the Basingstoke Canal.

Tunnel was only two miles away, but first there was the thrilling, unexpected sight of the remains of a castle, set back off the towpath. A West Highland white terrier, its nose stuck to some promising scent, rushed around. 'That's King John's castle,' its owner told me between puffs. 'They do say there's a tunnel from there to Odiham.' He told me the canal ended in a few hundred yards at Greywell Tunnel. 'He's filled in,' he said. For the moment, however, the tunnel could wait. Here were the remains of a castle, nearly eight hundred years old, all that remain from the place where King John left for Runnymede, about twenty-five miles away, to seal Magna Carta in 1215. I hung around for a while. Maybe it was on such a soft June day that King John rode to Runnymede. Greywell Tunnel was a few minutes away. Built *c*. 1792. 1,230 yards. The canal, heavily weeded, fades into the broken tunnel, impassable since a roof fall fifty years earlier which resulted in the final five miles to Basingstoke being abandoned and sold.

The Basingstoke Canal, opened in 1794, close to death's door in 1834, is generally regarded as having been a commercial failure. Well . . . no raging success anyway. It was one of those ventures that must have seemed a good idea at the time, a thirty-seven-mile link from Hampshire's agricultural heart to the edges of London. An agricultural canal, carrying produce one way and coal the other. A venture that failed. A failure predicted by one man who wrote to a magazine: 'The inhabitants of a little market town in Hampshire, where no considerable manufacture is carried on, having unaccountably conceived an idea that if a navigable canal was made "some way or other" from there to London, they should emerge from their present obscurity.' Only two years after the canal was opened, the company was on the verge of bankruptcy. But it survived, the canal being needed for the transport of materials in building the railway and Aldershot Camp in the mid 1800s. But financial problems were never far away, and the last barge to Basingstoke went in 1914 and the last commercial traffic of any sort in 1949. And the canal that seemed a good idea at the time was left in peace for a while. It must have suffered many indignities, not the least coming in 1957 when one of the locks at Frimley was partly blown up by troops returning from a night exercise. That must have been the limit.

Restoration, however, was just around the corner, and I could not help thinking how worthwhile it all was when I got back to Fleet and walked underneath spreading chestnut trees and enjoyed the sight of gardens reaching down to the canal. People do care, after all. The housing soon gives way to woodland, the woodland to the Royal Aircraft Establishment at Farnborough and a golf course, and all through lovely countryside. The presence of the Army is stamped on one pipe-carrying, barbed-wired bridge that declares: 'MOD property. Out of bounds at all times.' At Silvester's Bridge, the lads from a nearby barracks were jumping into the canal.

It was near here, at Ash Lock, that I witnessed a Tub Race, presumably for charity. One poor old bathtub trailed far behind the others, and when the cox tried to beat up some rhythm, he got a quick response. 'Do shut up, Gregory.' One of the mothers suggested they should sing something, but after a weary rendition of the opening line of 'Land of Hope and Glory', she revoked. 'Don't bother. Just paddle.'

There are splendid views from a high embankment over the Blackwater Valley, and around here the rhododendrons are particularly beautiful in another delightful stretch of canal. The waterway, heavily weeded in parts, might not be so good for people in boats but it is lovely walking country, wooded and peaceful. After only one lock in twenty-odd miles they start to come quickly together, with No. 20 bearing a plaque: 'Gates constructed by Royal Aircraft Establishment 1st Year Apprentices 1980.'

It was on this quiet section in the flight of Frimley Locks, some up to their knees in weeds, that I got a good, close look at a water vole having lunch. It was sitting up, like a squirrel, on a plank in the water, nibbling at a plant, shaving the leaves. As soon as it had finished, it dived into the water, found itself another plant and resumed eating on the plank. A jogger came along, and for a few minutes we stood and watched the vole, who was totally unconcerned by our presence and just carried on munching. Marine growth had also settled on the surface, and yellow water lilies were popping up. The variety of colour on the canal is remarkable with the different plant life, not to mention the butterflies and dragonflies zipping by.

Without realizing it, I had crossed into Surrey. A duck and seven ducklings made patterns in the marine growth, flags were flying from colourfully decorated and flowered houseboats, and there was Woking, one of London's thriving commuter towns. I sat for a few moments, on a bench that commemorates 'The Mayor's Canal Restoration Project 1982', and studied the office blocks and car-parks, the traffic whirling by and the collection of cranes in the town centre. Industry lingers on for a while, and the sounds of Woking force their way through the wooded path. The canal was now smothered in weeds but the woodland persists to make a pleasant walk past a sad, sorry, decaying old lock, dry and deep with weeds, and past a rope hanging from the branch of an oak tree, dangling on the path. The temptation was too great. I held on tightly, closed my eyes and swung out over the green slime of a patch of marine growth. I touched down on the towpath again with great relief. A lady in a slip of a dress passed by with a hotchpotch dog and carefully watched me. I smiled and hurried on, happy to see the canal regain some of its pride, and water, as it runs into the Wey Navigation. London is just around the corner.

DISTANCE OF WALK: 31 MILES.   **OS MAP 176 and 186**

Chelmer and Blackwater Navigation

It was a Sunday morning in spring. The time of year, the time of week, when the Essex countryside can be seen at its sleepy best. The day before had been beautiful, a welcome splash of sunshine in one of the wettest springs on record – 'a gorgeous day' according to the lady at my elbow at breakfast on the Sunday morning. The Sunday, however, was far from gorgeous. As I sat in the window of the Blue Boar at Maldon, stoking up on a boar-size breakfast, the rain started, the sort of apologetic drizzle that tempts you outside, gets you miles from nowhere, then drowns you.

Heybridge Basin at the start
of the Chelmer and Blackwater Navigation.

The Navigation link with the sea at Heybridge Basin is only about a mile from the Blue Boar. On one side of the thick, black lock a jumble of boats and ships wait for release from the clinging mud, some of them so old and tired they will never rise again. On the other side the still water of a canal, wide and busy, hundreds of yards of boats of all sizes, tall masts, ocean-going cruisers, catamarans and some little more than motor boats. From Ipswich and Hull, three and four deep, with a passage between. The Basin here is pleasant, with charming houses, the sight of the boats and two warm-looking pubs not surprisingly nautically named – the Jolly Sailor and the Old Ship.

I set off into the thunder and lightning of a storm which forced me to shelter under a bridge just beyond the village of Hayfield. The rain beat down, a million pin-pricks on the water, and I stood shivering under the bridge, huddled, looking back on the village of Maldon on the hill, a church tower peering above the trees, a small steeple standing high. A church bell tolled. I moved out, into surrounding land that is pleasing to the eye. Canary-coloured with the plant of the oilseed rape or green and lush, pastoral with hardly a sign of life.

I splashed on, through the double gates which are so much a feature of this path, through fields, past woods and the occa-sional glimpse of a farm building or cottage. I crossed a bridge and dropped back down to the towpath alongside a field of butter-cups, a host, a crowd of floating buttercups. This really is a river. Not a canal or a navigation but a country river, meandering, flowing thoughtfully with hardly any long, straight stretches. A true river, disorderly, eccentric, trees growing out of it, hedges dipping into it.

It was not long after twelve o'clock when I heard the sound of hymn-singing, reaching out for me down the towpath. I thought for one wonderful moment I had quietly passed on – washed on in my case – a blessed relief from the rain. But no. The lovely, sweet sound was coming from the little church of All Saints at Ulting on the other side of the river, isolated, right on the edge of the water, looking perilously close to falling in. But if it had stood there for seven hundred years, I guessed it could stick out another flood or two. I stood and listened and joined in. 'Bread of Heaven, Bread of Heaven, Feed me till I want no more, want no mo-o-o-o-o-re, Feed me till I want no more.'

Chelmer and Blackwater Navigation with the
13th-century church of All Saints at Ulting.

The Chelmer and Blackwater, opened in 1797 after years of planning to take a navigation to Chelmsford, has few road bridges crossing it, no villages directly on the path, no pubs that I could see after the Jolly Sailor and his Old Ship, only a few houses. I passed a sunken barge in the canal and another in a stretch of side water and felt again the depression I always get with sunken boats. I do hate to see them. It is the sight of something dying, I suppose. But in death there is always life, and with it came the wonderful sound of the cuckoo – my first of the spring.

The six hours of rain stopped as I reached the edge of Chelmsford, where I was due to watch a cricket match between Essex and Lancashire. By the time I arrived at the cricket ground, the sun was out, shining on the enormous lake that had developed where a cricket match should have been. The ducks had arrived. As I left the scene, I tried another chorus of 'Bread of Heaven'. Ulting church, I will not forget you. Dear little church, at the side of what is, despite the rain, a lovely stretch of water.

DISTANCE OF WALK: 14 MILES.   **OS MAPS 167 and 168**

The West

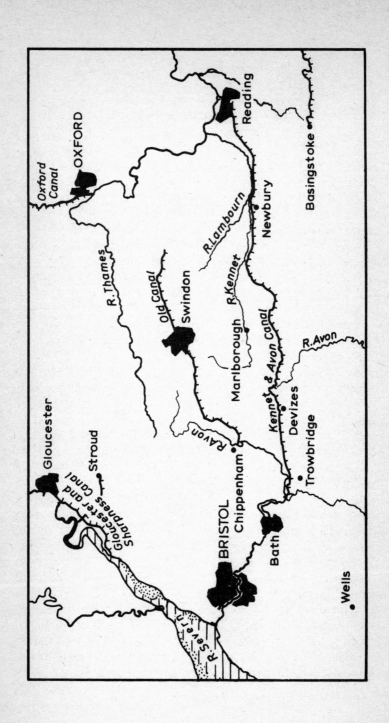

Kennet and Avon Canal

A little woman with fat legs and a big handbag in each hand picked her way towards me through the towpath puddles. Did I know where the big barn was. Had I perhaps passed it? It did stand on the side of the canal. I could not recall having seen any barns at all that morning, big or small, and as they are not the sort of thing you can overlook, I had to assure her she was heading in the wrong direction. I had crossed an aqueduct – well, two; I had seen the loveliest English countryside; I had just crossed the River Avon and seen a weir. But a big barn? No. She turned and left the canal at a nearby bridge.

I carried on round the southern edge of the town and there, as big as a church, was the great Tithe Barn of Bradford-on-Avon. I went inside through a huge, open, oak door into the vast emptiness of a building that has been standing six hundred years and is in perfect condition. I never fail to be filled with awe at such an experience, and for several minutes I could do little but stand and stare at a wonderful piece of the country's history. It was longer than a church – about half the length of a football field – and almost as high. The barn was bare; its four colossal doors had been thrown open wide, providing the only real light in the building. The only other light came from arrow slits high on the walls, including one like an enormous cross at the west end. The barn, once a granary for Shaftesbury Abbey twenty-five miles away, dates from the fourteenth century, with four gabled porches and fourteen great bays where wagons could be unloaded in the dry.

The barn was well over four hundred years old when the canal, connecting the Avon at Bath to the Kennet at Newbury, was completed in 1810. The two rivers had been navigable since early in the eighteenth century, and the canal, which linked Bristol and Reading, turned the whole thing into one of the foremost waterways in the south of England, 86½ miles long. The canal proper runs from one old town to another, from the noble Roman city of

The Roman baths and the abbey at Bath.

Bath to Newbury, the centre of the cloth trade in the Middle Ages. Bath stone, used extensively in creating crescents and squares and terraces in the city, was shipped down the Avon to Bristol or along the canal to Reading and the River Thames to London.

Bath is beautiful from any viewpoint. I stood on Camden Crescent, high up Lansdown Hill, and looked way, way down to the Avon in the valley and the canal just beyond it on the side of the hill. The waters join near the railway station at Widcombe Lock close to Halfpenny Bridge, a replacement for the original which collapsed in 1877 and sent a crowd of pedestrians plunging into the river. It cost a ha'penny to use the bridge, a fee that was collected in the small booth above the towpath. The Avon wanders off in the direction of the abbey under the Pulteney Bridge, lined with shops, the sort of elegant touch that a fine river deserves. There is no such handsome decoration for the canal, which has to be thankful for such attachments as the stone shell of the Thimble Mill pumping station and the unromantic-sounding Wash House Lock. Two tunnels were driven through Sydney Gardens, and on one of them stands Cleveland House, taken over by the canal company for their head office in 1825. A chute ran from the cellar of the house into a small hole in the tunnel roof, and messages and packets were dropped down through the chute from the canal office to the waiting boats.

Moving out of Bath, the majesty of the city opens out behind with its neat stone houses climbing the tree-topped hills. The towpath throughout makes for good walking, wide and green in parts, in keeping with a canal that spends almost all its time in the country. From Bath it is not far to Bathampton, where the dignified George Inn, considerably older than the canal, sits stolidly on the bank, making a lovely picture with the church in the background. Over the canal and the river, close together again as they take the sharp bend in the valley, I could see Batheaston church tower on the hill. I stayed in the village once, at the Old Mill Hotel, and was lulled to sleep by the sound of the river. There are benches on the towpath, ideally placed to appreciate the superb view through the valley. The canal clings to the hillside. Above is the main road to Warminster and below the railway line to Salisbury, and the Avon, heading for the ancient towns of Chippenham and Malmesbury. All share the wide, wooded valley. Across the waters is Warleigh Manor, covered from the waist up in red ivy. I could make out a colourful bank of flowers at the side with what looked like a conservatory behind, all set in trees and tucked into the hillside.

The valley swings to the right, and the road, the railway and the waters go with it, tight together like sardines in a can, past the beautiful Warleigh Wood. It really was a perfect day. Sunny, with a few wispy clouds looking out of place and with nowhere to go. A goods train trundled by as the canal approached Dundas Aqueduct which carries it over the railway and the river to the other side of the valley, close to Conkwell Wood. A Waterways Board man was tapping at the canal bank with a spade, showing the same sort of enthusiasm with which I set about the garden wilderness in spring. 'Canal's just about closed up for the winter,' he declared, leaning on the spade. 'Work can start now.' I thought I had better not hold him up and made for the sharp left turn across the aqueduct, named after the first chairman of the canal company. Here also was the entrance, now blocked, to the Somersetshire Coal Canal, opened in 1805 and abandoned ninety-nine years later. A striking picture of the aqueduct, in 1894, showing a barge going into the Somersetshire Coal Canal, with a railway engine down below, was used as the cover for Kenneth Clew's book on the Kennet and Avon Canal. Standing in just about the same place when I was there was a pleasure barge, the *John Rennie*, named after the canal's engineer.

The path, like the canal, changes sides, and once across the aqueduct it was to run alongside a bed choking with weeds and gasping for water. The scenery, however, is still delightful, with Monkton Combe and Limpley Stoke coming into sight, houses spotting the hillside across the valley, the river rippling its way through. The canal and the Avon turn their eyes to the east after Freshford, and the two waters again change sides at Avoncliff, a mile and a half below Bradford-on-Avon, the canal crossing the valley on a three-arched aqueduct, 110 yards long and of soothing, mellow Bath stone. I could see the path on the other side, but how to get there was a mystery. I took the simple way by crossing the canal bed, then asking a workman. 'No bridge, no. People get across on boards . . . don't seem to be no other way,' he said in the distinctive accent that reminded me I was in Wiltshire. I discovered the following day that the path changes over by running along a lane under the canal.

The river, after being close at hand since Bath, slides off to go through the fine old town of Bradford with its barn and its bridges and its precious little Saxon church. The canal, having regained water, stays aloof, above and on the edge of a town bursting with lovely buildings, including the Canal Arms and the Barge Inn! I stayed at the Swan in Bradford not so many years ago, a solid, aged coaching inn that still retained its ostler's bell and mounting block, and with a charming dining-room, low ceilinged and colour-washed, that looked to have changed little in 150 years.

About a mile and a half past Bradford, the Avon returns briefly to the canal as if it has forgotten to say goodbye. Then it charges north again, back to its birthplace. The railway, too, takes its leave, splitting north and south, and the canal is left to make its lonely way through the fields and the flatness to Semington and Devizes. Another junction is formed by the long-vanished Wiltshire and Berkshire Canal which ran for fifty-one miles to Abingdon and the Thames. The last traffic was in 1906, formal abandonment came in 1914, and the entrance takes some finding, near Semington Road bridge and on through somebody's orchard and garden.

A feature of this area, a repeat of the Basingstoke Canal, is the collection of pillboxes and tank-traps designed to keep Adolf Hitler at bay. Some have sprouted good heads of grass, another has burst open, its iron bars hanging out like entrails. Maybe the Germans got this far after all. But the towpath is lovely. Lovely country, lovely day, lovely walking, quiet, peaceful, with little more to talk to than the odd white goat, chewing the hedge.

Six locks, spaced out over half a mile, must have provided a good warm-up in the old days for the boatmen about to tackle the flight of seventeen up Caen Hill to Devizes. It must have been a daunting prospect. Large side ponds were built between the locks to act as reservoirs, and one of several improvements on the flight was the introduction of gas lighting in 1829. The canal company made its own gas at a works near the bottom of the hill, and an additional charge was made for boats travelling through at night. The run-down of the canal resulted in the flight being declared unsafe in 1951, the locks being padlocked and left to decay. Restoration is a big task, but when it is complete it will restore to the canal system the most impressive, spectacular flight of locks in the country. Just beyond the top lock is Prison Bridge –

Devizes

a prison once stood close by – and bearing a tablet: 'Erected by the Kennet and Avon Canal Company to the memory of John Blackwell who, during 34 years, superintended the works of the canal as their engineer with fidelity, vigilance and ability, 1840.'

Devizes is a dear old town, blessed with an array of historic buildings and a medieval street pattern in the shape of a fan with the castle at the bottom. The town claims there are nearly five hundred structures inside a quarter of a square mile worthy of some protection order, and also maintains that in eight hundred years not one new street line has been devised. In an age of demolition and precinct uniformity, these are astounding claims. The streets, I thought, twisted and turned back on themselves as I wandered up and around Monday Market Street, Snuff Street, the Brittox, Hare and Hounds Street, Sheep Street and Southbroom Terrace. But there is a pattern, even a simplicity about it

One of the thatched houses in Horton on
the Kennet and Avon Canal.

all. The buildings are a pot-pourri of styles with different heights,
designs, widths and colours. And keeping its distance on the top
side of the town is the relatively young Kennet and Avon canal
with its wharf where the Kennet and Avon Trust have a museum
and shop.

We – the canal, the path and I – did not take long to find the
fields again, roaming under hills with barrows and tumuli, the
occasional White Horse carved out of the side, and a neolithic
camp. The canal twists sufficiently to stay on the fringe of a
succession of small communities. The spire at Bishops Cannings
is passed on the left, Horton dozes on under its thatched roofs,
Allington and All Cannings are split by the canal, Stanton St
Bernard shows off its church tower in the trees, and Alton Barnes
stays far enough to the left. Then right out of nowhere comes
Honeystreet with the cream-coloured Barge Inn with picnic tables
and slumbering geese.

Picked Hill and Woodborough Hill, with farm buildings at its feet, dominate the scene as the water nears a fancy bridge at Cocklebury Farm, erected in 1808, prettily balustraded and fittingly called Ladies' Bridge. It was said that the landowner, Mrs Susannah Wroughton of Wilcot Manor, would allow the canal only if an ornamental bridge was built. Among the carvings on it is one by H. Smith, 2 December 1860. The first living thing I saw on the bank in hours was a water vole which strolled across the path, stopped at the water's edge, looked at me and then slid into the canal. The railway line from Newbury to Westbury brings new life and sounds, however, to the Vale of Pewsey, and from just after Pewsey village the two are to stay in sight of one another all the twenty miles to Newbury.

The great Savernake Forest lies to the north, but the hotel of the same name stands near the canal, over the five-hundred-yard long Bruce Tunnel, which runs under the down platform of the now closed Savernake low-level station. The path still took me under and alongside the railway and down a grassy lane across from the hotel. I knew I was back as soon as I saw the tank-traps at the head of the path leading to the canal, where a pheasant, apparently not used to intruders, ran along the path, like a frightened old lady, before finding an escape through the hedge. The top lock at Crofton was sadly filled with weeds and empty of water as the canal, just as straight as the railway, crossed the Roman Road – which goes through the Forest – and went on to Great Bedwyn, with its old thatched cottages and its large twelfth-century church, and Little Bedwyn. The A4, the main road from London to the West before the motorways arrived, joins up at Froxfield, and it was near here, at Barrackfield, that a swing bridge mysteriously disappeared for two weeks during the war. The United States Army returned it after borrowing it for use as a saluting base during an important review at a nearby camp.

The River Kennet, which takes over the navigation at Newbury, also comes close on the other side of Hungerford, a market town old enough to have been granted privileges by John of Gaunt in the fourteenth century. This is outstanding fishing country in extensive woodland, parkland and farmland. Kintbury, three miles from Newbury, was a busy spot a hundred years ago, with iron and coke deliveries to its wharf for five ironworks which made agricultural implements and machinery.

There was malt for the brewery and corn for the flour mill. And out went whiting, a fine powder, ground from chalk and used for making paint and whitewash. The Kennet and the canal, about to be married at Newbury, have a trial run near Copse Lock, a four-hundred-yard stretch where the river becomes the canal. But the Kennet and Avon becomes itself again to run into Newbury, past seventeenth-century weavers' cottages and up to a wharf that once handled a wide variety of produce, such as meal, timber, rope, tar and groceries, but which was filled in during the 1930s.

DISTANCE OF WALK: 57 MILES.   **OS MAPS 172, 173 and 174**

6

Gloucester and Sharpness Canal

Just when I thought I had finished with the Gloucester and Sharpness, when I was within sight of the docks jutting into the Severn at Sharpness, I stumbled on the most amazing scene in a thousand miles of towpaths – the burial ground for barges on the mud banks of the Severn. It is impossible to estimate accurately the number that have been driven to their deaths, grounded and stranded like whales. Forty or fifty, maybe more, some buried so deep that only their prows are showing, the rest of them covered in mud and overgrown with grass.

It is here that the canal, almost at the end of its near seventeen-mile run from Gloucester, slides alongside the Severn, mighty and wide although still miles from the Bristol Channel and the ocean. The canal, after running round the Wildfowl Trust at Slimbridge and through the charming village, the old port of Purton, swings left to keep company with the great River Severn. Only a spit of land about 150 yards wide separates the canal from the river, and it is here, across the water from the Forest of Dean, that the barges, among them the older and much larger Severn trows, have been laid to rest. The sight fascinated me. I hurried from one body to another, an intruder into grief. Not only have they been thrown up on the bank and left to die, they have had to make their own graves. A couple of concrete barges stand up defiantly, chests in the air, quite robust and healthy on the edge of the plague pit. Some of the remnants are just hulks, bones without flesh, several over a hundred feet long, the older Severn trows, strongly built sailing barges, the equivalents to the wherry and the keel from Norfolk and the Tyne or perhaps, nearer still, the Thames barge. I imagined them in the night, groaning in agony in their death throes, sinking a little deeper, thrusting their prows into the air, drowning men gasping for air, for life. The rudder of another reaches out pathetically for help.

This stretch of the Severn is called the Waste Weir. A British Waterways Board workman, on board a barge on the canal,

Barges left to die by the River Severn, close to Sharpness.

reckoned there must have been about fifty derelict boats, some of them completely buried and grass-covered. 'I have been working here thirty-four years, and just about all of them have been driven here in that time,' he said. 'When the Board of Trade would not pass them, they had to be dumped somewhere.' He described it all with the air of a farmer who nurtures and rears his livestock, then takes it for slaughter. It is just life . . . and death.

The Gloucester and Sharpness is a ship canal, the broadest and deepest in the world when it was completed in 1827, designed to bypass the dangerous tidal waters of the Severn. Originally, in the late eighteenth century, it was intended that the canal should run from Berkeley Pill – the water that runs into the Severn two miles downstream – to Gloucester, and until recently the canal was often referred to as the Gloucester and Berkeley. In fact, the Gloucester and Berkeley Steam Packet Company ran a regular packet-boat passenger service until just before the Second World War. Both docks at Sharpness and Gloucester are busy, thriving areas with cranes and warehouses, ships and boats and bustle and excitement, particularly at Gloucester where the beautiful Norman cathedral watches over from less than half a mile away.

It was a cold morning when I set off. I pottered round the dock area, enjoying its sights, its activity, the enormous range of craft. A dock policeman kindly guided me to the start of the towpath,

over a mile down the Bristol road where the canal comes into view
behind a timber yard. The road to Hempsted took me to the
bridge over the canal, clean, wide and impressive, full of itself, a
prince among canals in England, still carrying sea-going ships.
The cold wind blew straight down the water from Sharpness and
the Channel, through the industry that lines the banks. A white
iron mile post, three feet high, records the distance from Sharpness and Gloucester. It could not be more brief: 'S 14' on one side,
'G 2' on the other.

The first boat soon appeared, a chunky, cheeky-nosed affair
called *Trustee*, as industry fell behind and the Gloucestershire
country opened out. A notice on the use of the canal bank
proclaimed that, 'Use of a mechanically propelled vehicle or
horse-riding on any part of the towing path or bathing in any part
of the canal (including the docks at Sharpness and Gloucester) is
strictly forbidden.' And permits are needed for fishing – £3.50 for
the year, 60p a day (half price for children) and £1 to ride a bicycle
on the towpath.

Near Quedgley the river and canal come within shouting range
of one another for the first time since Gloucester. Quedgley
Wharf is the highest point reached by the oil traffic, and a notice
to shipping declares: 'To prevent damage to this wharf vessels
must stand clear when turning.'

There are sixteen swing bridges on the canal, all controlled by a
keeper and with a bridge-keeper's lodge, single-storeyed with
fluted Doric columns at the door. All very classy as if the Greeks
or Romans had taken a hand in the canal's construction. The
keeper at Quedgley told me the wharf, sprinkled with oil-
containers, handled five ships a week. 'There'll be one today,
about four o'clock,' he told me. 'Off to Sharpness? You've got a
nice day for it. Twelve miles from here. Say about three hours.'
Why is it, I thought, that everybody walks quicker than me.
Determined to step up my rate, I stepped out in lively fashion,
past Hardwicke and Moreton Valence, past the chalets in the
trees, alongside long, straight stretches of water, past the numerous scarred, white iron mooring stumps that litter the bank.

Soon after glimpsing the church tower of St Andrew's,
Wheatenhurst, among the trees across the water, I came to the
crosswater at Saul where the Stroudwater Canal crossed on its
way from the River Severn to the Thames and Severn Canal. The

locks on the towpath side linking the Stroudwater with the Gloucester and Sharpness look locked for ever. Long, husky arms reach out from the gates which look down on weeds ten feet high in the lock chambers. A sign on one of the gates reads: 'Built 1826', a year before the Gloucester and Sharpness was completed. The church clock clanked out the hour, a slow, dull ring that suited the sleepy surroundings. I hurried on, down the road on which the Waterways Board had warned motorists: 'Slow. 5 m.p.h.' That was slower than the boats, which are allowed to travel at 6 m.p.h. on this waterway.

The next bridge and road lead off to Frampton-on-Severn, a lovely, lovely, old village with a huge green, ponds and pubs, Georgian houses, half-timbered houses and a church in the meadows. As I walked away from the canal, I passed the entrance to the works on its banks. It belonged to Cadbury. 'Not any more,' a woman told me as I neared the green. 'It's been sold. Been there some years, too.' It must have been, for my grandfather travelled from Lancashire to Frampton to drive steam wagons for Cadbury just after the First World War. My mother remembers the green and the ponds, but the beauty of the place was not enough for my grandmother, who refused to leave her native Lancashire for the unknowns of Gloucestershire. Grandad had to go back home.

The outstanding house on the green is Frampton Court, screened by trees, built in the 1730s for Richard Clutterbuck, a Bristol customs official. I had the choice of two pubs, the Bell or the Three Horseshoes, next to the butcher's. I chose the Three Horseshoes and walked through the door straight to the bar. The total silence made me think I was alone until I turned and looked round to see one side of the room quite full. Nine men, all locals, were staring at the stranger at the bar. Once I had taken my drink and seated myself, near the window, conversation resumed. The topic, it seemed, was kidney beans, the mysteries of their sowing and cultivation. Somebody wrapped his in wet newspaper before sowing. The men, all retired, chewed this for a while. All went quiet for a minute before one, who looked like the pub elder, said in a soft, slow Gloucestershire burr: 'Seems to me there's more gardening done in here than anywhere.'

'I'm glad tomatoes have come to an end,' announced another. 'I'm fed up of eating the things.'

'Like me with my chickens,' said a man clutching his walking-stick. 'Don't much like eggs but I 'as to eat 'em when they lays 'em.'

I left the Three Horseshoes to its philosophies and its gardening and headed out of the village towards the lych gate that looked part of nowhere. Then I saw the church, six hundred yards away through an aisle of chestnut trees. Inside the porch is an Ordnance Survey map for 1955, the immediate area being almost entirely taken up by the River Severn with 'sand and mud' and the area called 'The Noose' as the river winds itself nearly into a circle.

Back at the canal I could now see the Severn and its Noose with the huge Forest of Dean beyond. And nearly five hours after leaving Gloucester I saw my first ship, the *Bisley* from London, incongruously chugging through the countryside with the church tower of Slimbridge, as thin as a pencil, coming into sight behind it. Several strange noises, none of which I could identify, from the Wildfowl Trust, were followed half an hour later by the banging and clattering of men hammering aboard a second ship, the *Trader* from San Lorenzo, as it passed close to the church and houses at the water's edge in Purton.

The coming of the canal turned Purton into a port with a customs house – next to the church – and river and canal pilots made their homes in the village which also used to have a pub called 'The Pilot'.

From Purton it is less than two miles to the docks at Sharpness. The canal, after heading straight for the river, turns sharp left to run alongside it, past the barges' burial ground, along to the huge, round stone tower on the towpath that supported the swing bridge that linked with the railway bridge across the Severn. The railway bridge took four years to build, was three-quarters of a mile long with twenty-one spans and was opened in 1879. A magnificent bridge. But in 1959, on a foggy November evening, two oil-tanker barges, nearing Sharpness Docks on the flood tide, became locked together and were swept up the river. One of the barges had an engine failure, and nothing could stop them careering on and into one of the bridge piers. One barge was loaded with petrol which became ignited and also set fire to the other barge, loaded with crude oil. The collision fractured the gas main which crossed the bridge, there was a terrific explosion, and

The superb dock area at Gloucester.

four of the eight crewmen on the boats were killed. The collision and explosions destroyed one of the largest spans, another was near collapse, and the two burnt-out barges were aground in mid-stream with part of the railway track between them. They are still there, still visible at low water. But the bridge itself has gone, taken down six years after the accident, but leaving the tower on the towpath, a reminder of a magnificent piece of engineering.

As the canal approaches Sharpness, the towpath swings sharp right towards the old dock and the stables for the towing horses. The last few hundred yards are taken up with boat and barge moorings but only yards away, over the wall separating the canal and river, are more barges, high on the bank, nose to tail, left to rot. I crossed the canal on the lock bridge, walked up the winding path, down the other side of the hill and through the new docks, past the timber yard and over the railway lines.

When the canal was built, Sharpness was just a rocky cliff jutting into the river, a wild and uninhabited area with the dockmaster's house and the stables being the only buildings. But with the new dock in 1874 came considerable life and a town that overlooks the canal and the river.

DISTANCE OF WALK: 17 MILES.   **OS MAP 162**

The South-West

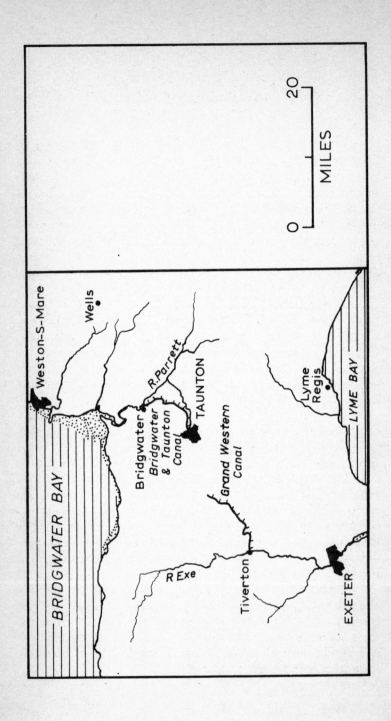

7

Grand Western Canal

A week or two earlier and instead of walking the Grand Western I would have been able to sample the old delights of sitting in a horse-drawn barge. No noise, no vibration, no fumes, just a smooth glide on the untroubled waters of a canal. Devon County Council have taken over the Grand Western and turned its entire eleven miles from Tiverton to Lowdwells into a country park. So even without the assistance of a boat this is none too taxing a stroll along the beautifully maintained canal and towpath through some delicious countryside with marvellous views. And no canal can have as many benches, most of them donated, for the weary.

I do not suppose the Grand Western was ever really all that grand. It would have been if it had come to full fruition and provided the navigation that was envisaged from the south coast to the north. The eleven-mile Tiverton bit was only a branch of the planned main line, opening in 1814 and providing transport for lime and roadstone from the quarries at Holcombe Rogus and Burlescombe to Tiverton. The building of the Bridgwater and Taunton Canal in 1827 renewed interest in the Grand Western, but it was still eleven more years before the branch was extended to Taunton, making 24½ miles in all. But that was the end of the Grand Western. The new section was closed in 1867 after a short life; the old section, Tiverton to Lowdwells, breathed properly again in 1971 when Devon County Council got to work and turned it into the little beauty it now is. Most of the towpath had been newly mowed, the hedges cut back, the weeds severely hacked, shortly before I was there. What it did for the wild life I do not know, but it worked wonders for the walker. It was a real joy. A lovely day's wander.

I lingered over the start, dallying around Tiverton, the first sizeable town in Devon the holidaymakers can hit on their way to Dartmoor and the Devon and Cornwall resorts. I enjoy everything about Devon, and I was in no particular hurry to move out of Tiverton, relaxed, slow-moving Tiverton, full of rich Devonshire accents and cream and warmth.

The start of the canal is, surprisingly, up a fairly long hill at the end of the town. Past the statue of Edward the Peacemaker (King Edward VII who died in 1910), the clock tower (1908) and the Prince Regent, then up, up, up Canal Hill. A sign – and you do not see many of those – points to the canal, and another, at the road entrance, pronounces it 'The Grand Western Canal Country Park'. A description of the canal greets you:

'The whole canal can be explored at leisure as it passes through attractive East Devon countryside. Eleven miles long, the canal runs from Tiverton to Lowdwells on the Somerset border. The towpath provides an easy walking route with opportunities for nature study, picnicking and fishing. The canal can also be explored from the horse-drawn barge during the summer. Built between 1810 and 1814, the Tiverton to Lowdwells section was to be part of a waterway link connecting the Bristol and English Channels. The Lowdwells to Taunton section was the only part of the link to be completed, opening in 1838 but abandoned and closed by 1869. The canal was used for conveying limestone from Burlescombe quarries to Tiverton where it was processed at the canal basin in the lime kilns which can still be seen. In 1848 the railway reached Tiverton and the canal, which was becoming increasingly expensive to maintain, declined and was virtually abandoned by 1924 after a major leakage had occurred. In 1971 it was acquired by Devon County Council from the British Waterways Board for use as a Country Park.'

There was still a little more uphill to reach the canal and the basin itself, a few steps to the water and a magnificent view over the rolling countryside. There were plenty of people about, strolling, children hell-bent for home after another hard day at school, several crossing the canal by way of the William Authers Bridge for the housing estate on the other side. Several lovely bungalows and houses give colour to the canal, with charming gardens that reach to the water, and although I had only just set off, I sat for a moment – on a seat in memory of Chris Grant, an angler – to drink in the scene. The seats are a feature of the canal for its entire length, one declaring, 'Happy Memories. Kit and Charles Cozens', one 'made and given by E. Batty 1975', another from George Mitchell in memory of his wife.

After about a mile the houses start to trail behind and the lovely land that is Devon unfolds. An aqueduct takes the re-born canal

The tea garden at Tiverton at the start of
the Grand Western Canal.

over a disused railway line, heavily overgrown with a path up the
centre, before it goes under the Tiverton-to-Taunton road,
sweeping wide to the left and passing a milestone that says
nothing more than 'III' – three miles from Tiverton. The canal
winds round and above Halberton, a lovely stretch with trees on
both sides, undisturbed peace with the only movement coming
from the raindrops as they fall from the leaves. Then I saw the
metallic blue flash of the kingfisher, my second that day after
having been on the Bridgwater and Taunton Canal in the morning. As the trees on the towpath side open out to well-trimmed
hedges, Halberton church tower comes into view, fronting a vista
of mile after mile of countryside. A perfect picture, precious,
indelible. The church, pressed in by trees, its windows blinking
in the face of the sinking sun, a ring of munching cows at hand.
The shadows from the trees steal across patchworked fields,
through honeycombed hedges, cloaking the sheep in the first
shade of evening. The camera shutter claps, catching an ageless,
unfading snatch of English life. This is the peace that men fought

for, the peace that belongs to every day and every person. This day it was mine.

The canal wanders along the side of the hill, and in the distance I thought I could make out the M5 motorway. What a contrast between the motorway signs and the milestones of the canal. Another appears near Sampford Peverell: 'VI'. That is all. VI from Tiverton. It was in the village of Sampford Peverell that several cottages were destroyed to make way for the canal, and it was here, during the 1811 cattle fair, that three hundred navvies, angry about the delay in receiving their wages, decided to riot. A house was attacked and one of the rioters was shot dead.

Night was settling in as I hurried on. At Ayshford I could hear a train rattling away on the valley bottom. Another bench, another giver, a lady called Louisa from Hastings. The quarries, which used to serve the canal, are evident now, and just off the road near Fossend Bridge are the remains of a priory. Soon after Waytown Tunnel the canal comes to an end at Lowdwells beside Lock's Cottage, the end of a quite lovely walk.

DISTANCE OF WALK: 11 MILES.   **OS MAP 181**

8

Bridgwater and Taunton Canal

If everything had gone according to plan, if the canal system had not been overtaken by railways and better roads, if life had not suddenly taken off at a hectic pace, the south-west corner of England would have a waterway from the north coast to the south. From the top of Somerset to the bottom of Devon. From the Bristol Channel to the English Channel. Somerset, Devon and Cornwall might never have spoken to the rest of us ever again. It was a grand plan, full of vision, that came to nothing. Although, to be fair, bits of it were constructed and bits of it remain, slices of canal that are now coming back to life in a beautiful part of the country. The River Parrett, the Bridgwater and Taunton Canal, the Grand Western Canal and the Exeter Ship Canal would have linked the channels. Today we are left with about thirty miles of that ambitious plan, with fourteen miles of the Bridgwater and Taunton, eleven of the Grand Western centred around Tiverton, and five miles of the Exeter Ship Canal.

It is difficult to think of another canal with more attractive towns at either end than the Bridgwater and Taunton, two Somerset market towns. Bridgwater, once a busy port until overshadowed by Bristol, now a hayseed of a market town; Taunton, sheltered by surrounding hills, blessed with fine buildings and watered, they say, with an abundance of cider. Enough, perhaps, to fill the canal to Bridgwater and bring life back to the deserted and forlorn dock area.

It is nineteen miles – by river – from Burnham-on-Sea to Bridgwater, and small coastal vessels still make the journey along the Parrett to the old port. Daniel Defoe, who visited the town in 1724, wrote of the tide of the river rising near six fathoms. 'Sometimes it comes in with such furious haste, as to come two fathoms deep at a time and when it does so, by surprise, it often does great damage to ships, driving them foul of one another, and often times oversetting them. This sudden rage of the tide is called the "bore" and is frequent in all the rivers of this channel, especially in the Severn itself.'

The dock was opened in 1841, when the canal, which ran from Taunton to Huntworth, two miles south of Bridgwater, was extended to the town itself. There were two basins, and so heavy was the traffic with schooners and sailing barges that it was possible to walk the two hundred feet across the basins on the decks of the craft. Today the dock is still intact but is sealed off from the river by concrete dams, and work to rebuild the smaller dock and develop the larger one on marina lines, has begun.

When I left Bridgwater at the start of the fourteen-mile towpath walk to Taunton, work was going on alongside the lock leading into the canal which started life at this end thick with the seed of marine growth and a goodly variety of rubbish. Soon I was walking between high, red sandstone walls. Flowers peeped over the top; starlings popped out of wind-blown holes in the wall, the red of which contrasted pleasantly, almost vividly, with the green of the water.

A man, old and stooping, walked the path with his terrier. 'Nobody seems to bother about this canal,' he said. 'Wants taking in hand. Goes quite a way, you know. Up to Somerset Bridge. No, past there. Let's see. Tum Moorland. That way.'

The canal, in fact, goes far beyond Somerset Bridge and Moorland, winding its way round Bridgwater for half a circle, behind neat houses and gardens, cabbage patches and roses, heading for the M5 motorway and open country. I sheltered from the rain under the bridge and listened to the motorway traffic rumbling and rolling and rattling overhead. Just beyond is the Boat and Anchor Inn with Cinderella's Disco, and to the left, standing high and proud in the flat of the moors, is the lovely fifteenth-century tower of the village church in Westonzoyland, around where was fought the Battle of Sedgemoor in 1685, the last battle worthy of the name to be fought on English soil. Not many years earlier I had been to the village, to the site of the battle, into the church where prisoners were held, into the pub called Sedgemoor where marks on the side of the original stone fireplace were said to have been caused by the sharpening of weapons before the battle. I looked again over the vast flatness of the moor, searching out Chedzoy in the north and Middlezoy to the south, and recalled . . .

King Charles I had been executed, Oliver Cromwell and King Charles II had died and Charles's brother had taken the throne as James II. But an illegitimate son of Charles, the Duke of Monmouth, decided to claim the throne from his uncle with an army composed mainly of peasants, brave but poorly armed. His attempt failed at Sedgemoor, where a monument now declares: 'To the glory of God and in memory of all who doing the right as they saw it fell in the Battle of Sedgemoor 6th July, 1685, and lie buried in this field or who for their share in the fight suffered death, punishment or transportation.'

I stepped gingerly about the churchyard, trying hard not to disturb the peace of the eleven royal soldiers buried there. Sixteen of the King's soldiers were killed nearby, and the other five were buried inside the church, where a framed account of the church's part in the battle tells that five hundred rebel prisoners were brought into the church, seventy-nine wounded, five dying of their wounds. At the Bloody Assize which followed, Judge Jeffreys ordered the execution of about 330 rebels. More than eight hundred were transported to Barbados, and thirty-four were whipped. Many local peasantry fought with the rebels, using improvised weapons, and the swinging sign outside 'The Sedgemoor' portrays one royal cavalryman facing peasants in smocks with scythes and even a pitchfork. Royal troops are believed to have stayed at the inn, and the landlord told me it was a local tradition that the marks on the fireplace were caused by them sharpening their swords. He thought it more likely that locals had sharpened their scythes there . . .

I shook the memories out of my brain and continued along the canal path – excellent from start to finish – to a stretch, so popular that the owners of a house near the water's edge had warned: 'No picnicking, no fishing, no parking in front of house.' Their patience had clearly been tested to the limit. Another sign had been erected: 'For sale.' There was little life, however, near a canal which spends nearly all its life in the country, and I got extra pleasure from the sight of a kingfisher, its shiny, metallic blue back sparkling as it skimmed away.

The village of North Newton marks the halfway stage of the canal. The water in nearby locks, with their concrete arms, bubbled away like geysers as the rain beat down on two anglers huddling together underneath one of those enormous spreading umbrellas that look big enough to shelter the entire population of the village. A heron which had kept me company for two or three

Firepool Lock at Taunton.

miles, always keeping at least fifty yards ahead, at last decided it was time to leave. As it flew on to the path allowed me just a little nearer, then flew off over the trees and the railway line which accompanies the canal for almost the entire fourteen miles. There was more wild life to compensate for the lack of people. A squirrel ran across a field to an oak tree, and I was attracted by the white, bobbing tail of a rabbit as it moved among a herd of cows which took no notice whatsoever of the little intruder. A swan enjoyed itself by rushing up the canal, flapping its wings, skidding to a halt, then turning round to repeat the performance.

The village of Creech St Michael, three miles from Taunton, has grown in recent years with more housing, but it is still worth leaving the canal for a few minutes just to wander down the hill to the thirteenth-century church. It was around here that another old canal ran to Chard thirteen miles away, a waterway which survived only twenty-six years in the middle of the last century.

The town of Taunton opens up as the canal again crosses under the M5 motorway, its several churches dutifully reaching for the sky. The railway station, which marks the end of the canal, comes into view before the water runs away through the lock at Firepool, lowered into the River Tone, itself once navigable right back to Bridgwater.

DISTANCE OF WALK: 14 MILES.   **OS MAPS 182 and 193**

The Midlands

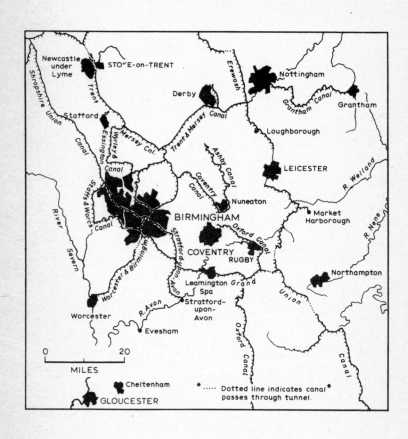

Newcastle under Lyme
STOKE-on-TRENT
Derby
Erewash
Nottingham
Grantham Canal
Grantham
Shropshire Union
Trent
Stafford
Essington
Wyrley &
Canal
Mersey Cnl.
Trent & Mersey Canal
Loughborough
Staffs & Worcs Canal
River Severn
Coventry Canal
Ashby Canal
LEICESTER
R. Welland
Canal
Nuneaton
BIRMINGHAM
Oxford Canal
Market Harborough
R. Nene
COVENTRY
RUGBY
Worcester & Birmingham
Stratford-upon-Avon
Leamington Spa
Grand
Northampton
Union
Worcester
R. Avon
Stratford-upon-Avon
Oxford Canal
Evesham

0   20
MILES

Cheltenham
GLOUCESTER

······ Dotted line indicates canal passes through tunnel.

9

Oxford Canal

The Oxford Canal, like a flighty young maid, runs hand in hand with the main London-Scotland railway line for a few miles before sharply breaking off the affair to head across country for the line to Oxford. They meet at Fenny Compton, near the George and Dragon, and are soon running south together, the railway smoothly heading straight for his goal, the canal skipping and dancing her way through the fields, through the green of the Oxfordshire countryside. Somehow they reach Oxford together.

I last walked the towpath of the Oxford Canal in autumn. Not quite the autumn of drifting leaves, but the autumn of misty mornings, the first chill in the air, the first suggestion of the changing season. It was just after seven in the morning when I drove down the lane to Hawkesbury Junction, near Coventry, carefully feeling my way over the lumps in the road, the 'dead policemen', and turned into the yard of Mike Walder's pub on the water's edge, the Greyhound Inn. Dawn was just rubbing the sleep out of its eyes, opening them to a chalky, grey morning with the treetops sitting like black balls of wool on the mist. The jagged line of the less fortunate, lifeless, leafless trees stood out against the grey. House lights shone out, diffused. It felt like November, even February, instead of the first day of October.

Here is the junction with the thirty-eight-mile long Coventry canal; 'a sad and melancholy spot' is how it has been described since it lost the bustle that marked it when barges lined up waiting for work from the nearby collieries. But I found it fascinating, with the Greyhound sitting on the hairpin bend at the joining of the waters.

The Knave of Clubs was already going through the shallow lock, and three tousled-haired lads were settling into the best seats on the bank, loading their hooks, oblivious to the morning chill. A convention of pylons jumbled together, sizzling and hissing angrily as they looked over to the Elephant and Castle, to the sunflowers in a garden across the water which were understandably starting to hang their heads, bowing to the coming cold. A grey squirrel bobbed down the path ahead of me, stopping periodically to make sure I was following. I would not have been at all surprised if it had produced a watch out of its waistcoat pocket and exclaimed: 'Oh my ears and whiskers. How late it's getting.' But it was only just after 7.30, and after a few minutes the squirrel turned off into the trees.

The sound of the traffic from the M6 motorway rumbled as I walked over Wyken Arm, once part of the original line and now used as moorings. After an hour of motorway thunder the sound begins to recede as the canal mosies its way through the village of Ansty with its road, cottages, houses by the water. A narrowboat, *Eroica*, optimistically advertised: 'P and O Cruises to the sun' on one of its windows. An inter-city train on the main Euston-Glasgow line hooted upwater, and a flock of pigeons rose. The canal made straight for the M6 again, and I could just make out the traffic at the edge of the mist, slow-moving animals, some humpbacked, some low and sleek and slightly sharper.

My book on the canal suggested a shallow depression, the track of the old canal, in a neighbouring field. I peered through the greyness. No depression except, perhaps, on the motorway where yellow lights twinkled in the gloom. Roadworks, no doubt. The path here becomes boggy and virtually non-existent for two hundred yards but soon recovers to accompany the canal and the railway under the M6 – before deteriorating again. The next section is marked by cast-iron roving bridges which used to carry foot traffic over the canal which wound its tortuous way through the fields before being shortened by fourteen miles in 1834. One of the bridges has deep grooves in its arm rail, criss-crossing like a girl's plaits and in places almost eating a way through the iron, forming a channel for the rainwater.

At the approaches to the village of Newbold-on-Avon lies the Newbold tunnel, 250 yards long, a part of the canal-shortening operation 150 years ago. It is dark and forbidding, with a hand-railed towpath on both sides. Ivy, brambles and wild roses dangle over the entrance to the tunnel. The rust on the handrail crumbled under my left hand, my right reached out for the wet, clammy, sloping wall. I resisted the temptation to run, but walked briskly towards the light and the narrowboat at the other entrance, *L'Escargot* from Rugby. Near the canal, the Boat Inn and the Barley Mow, both of which served meals, were preparing to open.

The first of my two offers of lifts came on this stretch, from *L'Escargot* as it drifted towards me. 'Jump on. But don't blame me if you fall in.' The man was alone. 'I've had the boat for ten years. We were going to have a fifty-footer but we were advised to get as big a boat as we could afford. The Leeds and Liverpool Canal has a limit of sixty-two feet for the locks, so we settled for this, sixty feet. I'm usually out over the weekend. I left last night, going back for dinner now, watch television this afternoon.'

'You must get to know a lot of people?'

'Not know them, no. I do get to recognize the boats, though. We know each other by the names of our boats. I'm Mr L'Escargot.'

Mr L'Escargot stopped after half an hour, alongside the golf club and not far from the wireless transmitting station at Rugby. 'Time for dinner.'

At Hillmorton Locks a map points out just about everything in the village that the traveller might need, a chip shop, launderette, chip shop, Stag and Pheasant, hairdresser's, ironmonger's, post box, Church of St John the Baptist, chip shop. I smiled pleasantly at Mr Popalong and Mr Amazing Grace II as I took off for the Royal Oak and a half-hour's rest. The towpath was getting hard work, uneven and overgrown, and I was tempted to thumb a lift when I saw Mr Popalong catching up. But there was only Mrs Popalong aboard. Not quite the thing. The path becomes worse as the canal village of Braunston approaches, long, tedious stretches of thick undergrowth with wild rose, hawthorn and bramble bushes tearing at my clothes and face, impenetrable in places and forcing me into the adjoining field.

The junction with the Grand Union canal is marked by two iron bridges from Horseley Iron Works with a brick bridge between, and as I swung right, past the Boat Shop, I peered in through the passing windows of Mr Bindweed and Mr Water Ouzel. The path is reluctant to improve over this remote, unpeopled area, and I was again forced to leave it, once for total escape through the tiny village of Lower Shuckburgh before reaching the loneliness of Napton Junction, twenty-eight miles from Hawkesbury, forty-nine from Oxford.

After a night with Hugh and Judy Bankes-Price at their 'spuds

War memorial and Victorian church of St John the
Baptist at Lower Shuckburgh in Warwickshire.

and wheat' farm near Stockton, I resumed the following day, a Sunday, picking up the canal under the hill on which stands the enchanting village of Napton. The canal winds its way around the hill, through nine locks and watched just about the whole way by the early nineteenth-century windmill, standing on the crown of the five-hundred-foot hill, one of the highest spots for miles around. From there, the locks reach into the deep south of Warwickshire, touching the border villages of Marston Doles, Priors Hardwick and Wormleighton.

The grey of Saturday had given way to a bright, blue Sunday, warm and sunny and inviting. The canal stirred with life. The smell of breakfasts wafted down the water from the flotilla of barges preparing for the day. People on the boats exchanged greetings with the people on the banks, and there was a happy bustle about the place, a day to look forward to. It was a lovely morning. The windmill stood high to the left with the sun at its side, pale and spreading, so watery you could almost look it in the eye.

Some Americans offered me a lift but I declined. They still had the nine locks to get through, and I thought it might delay me. The man in front, Mr Hyperion, leaned lazily on the rudder, enjoying a mug of tea, while his wife pressed on to open the next lock, the next set of paddles. She looked to have got into a fast, rhythmic pace. I asked if she was sure she had the work allotment right. 'Actually, I'm better at it than him,' she said. 'He tends to wander round wondering what to do next.' Clever fellow.

I was soon deep into the countryside again, but with it came a path so difficult to keep to that I cut across the fields by public footpath. As I went, I heard the church bell ringing to the east. But where? Priors Hardwick, Upper Boddington, Priors Marston? I could not tell. But what did it matter? The sound was lovely.

The canal writhes like a snake here as it finds a way round Wormleighton Hill, and it twists so much that two bridges a little over half a mile from each other over the hill are two miles apart by water. As I headed purposefully for the wharf at Fenny Compton, a small woman, grimly hanging on to a lead and a straining hound, quickly inspected me, my boots, cords, rucksack, the waterproof fastened round my middle. Her accent was Scots, her wit dry and cutting. 'Looks like Everest or bust . . .'

The canal enters a cutting at Fenny Compton, still known as 'The Tunnel' although it was opened out by the canal company in the middle of the last century. Walking was not easy, so I took to the neighbouring road into Claydon just inside the Oxfordshire border, a sleepy spot where all the life seemed to be concentrated in the pub, the Sunrising. The church stands next door, perhaps the oldest in the county, with a saddleback tower and a clock that still strikes the hour after three hundred years, but which has no face. This is England. A village on a hill with a charming church and busy pub, sheep and cattle around, a solitary road winding up the hill. A farm now stands where once was a Gilbertine priory; in the distance I could make out two more farms, a triangular spread of trees, brown, green and golden fields, and the only noises were those of the country – farm machinery, the wind rustling the trees and grass, a dog barking, a bird singing. I looked down on a narrowboat edging along the canal, loafing along. Everything was timeless.

I made my way back to the towpath and along to the lock at Cropredy, the scene of a Civil War battle in 1644. King Charles slept in the manor house after the battle, and the church contains relics of the battle, including suits of armour, cannon balls and swords. They do say that the brass eagle lectern was hidden in the River Cherwell at the time, so it would not be damaged by the soldiers. When it was recovered, one of the three brass lions at the foot of the pedestal was missing. Another was made, not of brass but of bronze, leaving two lions shining brightly, one dull.

Three more locks before Banbury: Slat Mill, Little Bourton and Hardwick. The traffic was thinning as much of it settled itself for the night. A retriever dog came running along the path, bounding along as it accompanied a boat. A little further along I almost stepped on a frog, lying on its back. It was feebly kicking its legs, and it was crying. I put it into the canal and did not see it again.

Industry marks the approach to Banbury, and when Marks & Spencer hove into sight, I knew I had arrived. But where is the old cross? Destroyed by the Puritans nearly four hundred years ago. And the fine lady upon a white horse, with rings on her fingers, and bells on her toes? Sadly, nowhere in sight. And the olde, originale Banbury Cakeshop, surely that is still here? But no, all gone, sir, all gone. I decided to move on. On to my cock-horse and out of today's Banbury. Oxford was beckoning.

The River Cherwell, which joins the canal for company up above Cropredy and which becomes the canal itself for a short while, was still around, usually the middle man with the railway on the other side. When I took off for Kings Sutton, I crossed them both, heading for the impressive church steeple. This is a lovely section of the canal, wooded, the river at its side, trees, including some wonderful old conker trees, overhanging the water. Kings Sutton, refreshed by the rain, was beautiful with its green, the stocks, thatched houses, black and white timbered, butcher's shops, pubs, the parish church of St Peter and St Paul. The main street coils its way down past the brass lanterns and the night nurse's house – 'Please do not knock – night nurse sleeping.'

Meanwhile, back on the canal, the water passes under Nell Bridge and through the lock, under the main London–Banbury road with one of the waterway's oldest bridges beneath the newer part of the bridge. Villages and hamlets abound on either side of the canal which settles into a good, walking towpath, at times almost in the country as the canal wanders river-like through the meadows. Somerton, Steeple Aston, Upper and Lower Heyford, Nethercott and Tackley, Kirtlington and Bletchingdon. It is around Bletchingdon that the Cherwell takes over for about a mile, the path being separated by weeds and reeds from the water, which gets ever wider, more ambitious and beautifully rural before being brought back to earth with a bang: Oxford Canal to right. Past Shipton Weir Lock and over the footbridge to the other side to walk between the waters again.

It is here, where the railway crosses over the canal and the Cherwell, that nine carriages crashed into the canal on Christmas Eve 1874. Standing there, in the clear daylight more than a hundred years on, it seemed remarkable that thirty-four people should have perished in the accident. Even more astonishing that two of the bodies, both children, should never have been claimed and were buried in the nearby Hampton Gay churchyard, where, so I had read, a gravestone commemorates the people who were killed. At the next bridge I left the canal, crossed the river by the footbridge and walked over the bumpy field, a remnant of the medieval ridge-and-furrow method of farming, to the railway line and the tiny church of Hampton Gay, alone in a field with the ruins of the Jacobean manor house 150 yards further on. The

Oxford Canal, with one of its attractive little drawbridges.

church door was locked, and hard though I tried, I could find no mention of the accident. Just one headstone: 'In affectionate remembrance of Benjamin, the beloved son of William and Elizabeth Taylor of Wolverhampton, Staffordshire, who departed this life December 24th, 1874, aged 19 years.' I wondered . . . a university student on his way home for Christmas? Another sad epitaph stands near the church door, a small stone commemorating a beloved son, died 1980, aged twenty months – 'a beautiful, sunny-tempered little boy.'

The canal bends like an elbow at Thrupp past the Boat Inn and the Jolly Boatman, then runs alongside the Wise Alderman at Kidlington, pubs all so different in character, one a local, one keeping everybody quiet with a nice brisk trade in meals, the other a hearty, country, boaty type of a place.

Three miles before Oxford is the Duke's Cut, a short cut through to the Thames which was dug at the request of the fourth Duke of Marlborough to link up with Wolvercote paper-mill. The suburbs of Oxford are around, and soon the first church spire of the city can be seen. The last stretch is a perfect finish, with the canal on the left and the Thames (or Isis, as it is also called) on the right. The last boat, as the Oxford Canal reaches its dead end against the bridge wall, was called *Mandingo*. I wondered if it had heard of my Mr L'Escargot.

DISTANCE OF WALK: 77 MILES.   **OS MAPS 140, 151 and 164**

End of the Stratford-upon-Avon Canal, close to the
Royal Shakespeare Theatre and the Shakespeare Monument
in Bancroft Gardens.

10

Stratford-upon-Avon Canal

Few canals have such a perfect ending as the Stratford, running into the River Avon in one of England's loveliest and best-loved towns. It creeps into the town almost unnoticed behind hedges and walls, but ends in a blaze of glory in the heart of the visitors' Stratford, close to the Royal Shakespeare Theatre and right next to the Shakespeare Monument in Bancroft Gardens. The canal is only twenty-five miles long, connecting with the Worcester and Birmingham at King's Norton, six miles out of Birmingham. It was constructed in two sections, the northern part from King's Norton to Lapworth, where it joins with the Grand Union, coming first in 1803, with the southern half following thirteen years later. Today, the canal is run as two distinct halves, the north belonging to the British Waterways Board, the south, with its entry into Stratford, to the National Trust.

The split is evident to the walker, along a difficult or non-existent towpath in parts in the north, better maintained in the south. Happily, I started at King's Norton and soon got the worst parts behind me. If I had been in a boat, I am sure I would have regarded it more appreciatively as the canal finds its way through the Birmingham suburbs for the first five miles. The city is well hidden behind hedges and trees, leaving the canal unexpectedly quiet and, in parts, untouched. But for anybody on foot it has spells of hard work and at times is impassable.

It was a lovely warm day when I experienced the canal, peaceful and still and a welcome change after a month of rain. A dog was swimming in the water, the white hawthorn blossom was beautiful, and children were enjoying the change of weather, swinging across the canal by a rope attached to the guillotine stop lock at the start of the canal at King's Norton. The lock, designed to prevent water supplies going from one canal to the other, comprises two wooden gates in iron frames. They have been permanently raised for thirty-five years and were proving a good playground for the children, who were also trying desperately to get some movement out of the seized-up machinery. Within a mile the path gets difficult, forcing me to scramble up the side of the banking, then wishing I had stayed to fight it out at the water's edge. My discomforts contrasted with the relaxations of a man on a boat peacefully reading his magazine who waved lazily as I blundered on, charging down the hill only to find the path led up again to go over the 322-yard Brandwood Tunnel. The old horse-path has vanished but I soon found my way back to the canal, to the singing birds, smiling red campions and stinging nettles. The going is hard with the path close to the water but the surroundings are delightful.

A man and woman, sweating even more than me, were looking for a big black dog that had jumped off their boat. A few minutes later a boy on the other side of the canal asked if I had found my black dog. I was getting quite concerned about the animal, but I had enough problems of my own, scrambling along the path, ducking and weaving to avoid the bushes and making sure I did not fall into the water. Then I saw it – a big black dog, patiently sitting by the side of a moored boat.

Once clear of the Birmingham suburbs, the canal experiences the countryside proper as it meanders through fields, the quiet of the day being disturbed only by the flap of birds' wings, the sound of sheep or a tractor in the distance, and the occasional cuss from me when I was wounded yet again. The towpath is slow to improve. Nettles and weeds are so high I felt like a soldier hacking a way through the jungle. Bushes were still pushing me dangerously close to the water, and in the end I gave in to the non-existent path and escaped to the road at Salter Street where the church bells were ringing merrily. The road leads to the Bull's Head, a lovely old country pub with a water pump in the garden. The road runs close to the canal for long sections to Lapworth and the start of the locks that lead to the connection with the Grand Union and to the National Trust's part of the Stratford Canal. As I walked past Lapworth, the village cricket team were playing, right next to the canal. The following day I would be at the World Cup. Today I would sit under an oak tree on a beautiful, sunny day and sample the pleasures of village cricket with its small pavilion, well-mowed, cared-for field and spectators dozing in deckchairs.

The lock area around Lapworth and Kingswood is interesting

William Shakespeare Monument in Stratford-upon-Avon.

and beautiful. Here are two unique, charming features of the
Stratford Canal with its split bridges and barrel-roofed cottages.
Several bridges, with a one-ton limit, were constructed with a
one-inch split through the middle so the towing line could pass
through without being unhitched. A notice on the Canal Office
wall referred to licences needed for boats travelling on the Stratford Canal and River Avon – £15.50 each for the Lower Avon

(Tewkesbury to Evesham), Upper Avon (Evesham to Stratford) and the canal. All three were available for £40 for fifteen days. A collection box on the wall was accompanied by a notice: 'After 50 years of dereliction this canal was restored (1961–64) by volunteers, prisoners and servicemen with the help of subscribers. Upkeep costs are heavy. Will you help?'

I set off for Stratford, passing a cottage displaying traditionally painted gifts such as metal jugs, teapots, bells and plant-holders. The walking had become much easier. The countryside is relaxing and rolling, with fields and hedges, chimneys peeping over the hills, families of ducks and moorhens, here and there a farm or an old barn. A stream ripples, trees creak in the breeze, smoke drifts on the air.

The Haven Tea Room, a popular eating place when we holiday near Stratford, is on the canal bank at Preston Bagot; an iron trough aqueduct sits on girders and brick pillars to straddle the Birmingham–Stratford road at Wootton Wawen. An isolated lock known as Odd Lock leads into another iron tank of an aqueduct, the impressive Edstone, 475 feet long and standing high over two railways, a road and a stream with the towpath carried below the water. I was soon at Wilmcote, the home of Shakespeare's mother, Mary Arden, and close to the top lock in the Wilmcote flight of eleven which starts the canal on its descent to Stratford and the River Avon.

The towpath had the last word as it neared Stratford, being muddy and overgrown in one part and underwater, forcing me to wade, as it went under the railway line. It looked a lot smarter when it became part of somebody's garden, forcing walkers to go between onions on the right, poppies and marigolds on the left. There is no towpath under the bridge leading into the basin, so I left after the fifty-fifth lock and walked along the road to Bancroft Gardens, the theatre and the monument. A perfect ending to the day.

DISTANCE OF WALK: 25 MILES.   **OS MAPS 139 and 151**

11

Worcester and Birmingham Canal

For the millions of chocolate-lovers in this country, there can be no fairer walk in all England than down the Worcester and Birmingham Canal. There is no need to walk all its thirty miles, no real need to see its five tunnels or its fifty-eight locks, no call really for any great exertion at all. Just amble forwards and backwards through Cadbury's works at Bournville, the Birmingham suburb four miles from the city centre. And as you go, breathe deeply. It is a wonderful experience, quite free of charge and fairly tantalizing, too.

Cadbury's have not only manufactured chocolate. They manufactured a village, a clean, crisp suburb of Birmingham, tree-lined and spacious. It all seems to have been the brainchild of George Cadbury, a partner with brother Richard in the manufacture of cocoa and chocolate. In 1879 they moved their business from the centre of industrial Birmingham to a rural area four miles to the south-west near the Bristol road. George believed that the root of most social evils lay in bad housing conditions, and as soon as the new factory was established he bought land in the neighbourhood and began to build Bournville village. By 1900 – five years later – the estate covered 330 acres and there were three hundred houses. He then handed the whole property over to a body of trustees, the Bournville Village Trust, on behalf of the nation, ensuring that all profits should go to the development of the estate and promotion of housing reform.

Mr Cadbury should see Bournville now. More a small town than a village, well ordered, a development of which he would have been proud. I was there when the workforce was arriving, hundreds of them. I suppose thousands. They poured out of the railway station and off the buses, the villagers walked in, the cars swept in. Notices asked drivers to use the car-parks provided and not to park around the green.

The canal, of course, had been there a year or two before George and Richard Cadbury arrived. Authorized at a cost of

£180,000 in 1791, it was not completed until 1815 with the spending of £610,000, running from the heart of industrial Birmingham to the rather more rural surroundings of the River Severn at Worcester. It was originally intended that the canal would take the great Severn barges, the trows, but although two barge locks were built at Worcester, the other fifty-six were much more modest. So much for the best-laid schemes o' mice and canal-builders. Most of the trade came from building materials, chemicals, coal, wood, limestone and salt, a good deal of it through the Droitwich Junction Canal when it was completed in 1853. There was general merchandise, too, which should have included the odd tin of cocoa or bar of chocolate, and it is thought that deliveries to the Cadbury factory were among the last on the canal in the early 1960s.

Wherever possible I try to finish my days out somewhere pleasant. If it can possibly be beautiful, so much the better. It makes the whole day that much more worthwhile and helps clear the weariness. So where was it to be, Birmingham or Worcester? For somebody who has never been able to come to terms with Birmingham city centre – I once went round the Bull Ring for two days – and who adores just about everything to do with Worcester, the choice did not create too many headaches.

I left Birmingham Gas Street Basin, or Worcester Bar as it is also known, at daybreak. Here is the centre of the Midlands canal network, joining the Birmingham Navigation network, although for several years up to 1815 a barrier stopped boats running from one canal into the other. This was the 'Worcester Bar' and meant that goods had to be unloaded there, transported a short distance to the other side of the barrier, and re-loaded. This was at the wish of the Birmingham Canal proprietors to preserve water. Perhaps they feared the competition, too.

My first intention was to run as hard as possible and leave Birmingham city centre far behind. But the way out is surprisingly pleasant, urban yet rural, as the canal steals its way out to the country through Edgbaston and its short tunnel, Selly Oak and Bournville, of course. I slid past the Botanical Gardens on the right, the ancient and modern of Birmingham University, set in parkland, on the left, and the Queen Elizabeth Hospital. The remains of a railway line at Bournville belonged to Cadbury's and was a connection between the factory and warehouses and the main railway line. The main railway line to Worcester and Cheltenham runs so close, in fact, that I could have done the first three miles by train, watching the towpath from a comfortable seat at least as far as Bournville. Just beyond, the canal and railway separate, going their own ways for about twelve miles before joining up again above Droitwich.

I pottered around Bournville for a while, savouring that lovely feeling of watching other people off to work before rejoining the canal and heading for the junction with the Stratford-upon-Avon Canal at King's Norton. The steeple of St Nicholas medieval parish church looked particularly striking as I walked the path I had first taken some months before when I set off from King's Norton for Stratford. I remembered how difficult some of the walking had been at this end of the Stratford Canal. The Worcester and Birmingham was to be just as hard around King's Norton, and after a fifteen-minute battle with the undergrowth, including the rubbish thrown over the back fence and into the cutting, it was a relief to reach the steps leading up and away from Wast Hill tunnel.

'Wast Hill Tunnel. 2,493 metres.' Why could we not keep to our own lovely yards and furlongs and chains and things? About a mile and a half I should think, the longest tunnel on the canal and, if my reckonings are correct, the fourth longest still in regular use, behind Dudley, Blisworth on the Grand Union, and Harecastle on the Trent and Mersey. The severe winter of 1978 brought problems and closure to a tunnel which was getting on for two hundred years old, and in the following year, during reconstruction, there was a roof collapse and two workmen were killed. The tunnel re-opened in 1981. The path along which the horses were led has been partly consumed by a housing estate, but it was fun finding the way, looking for clues and eventually finding the other end. At the King's Norton end of the tunnel I passed numbers 1 and 2 Tunnel Cottages before choosing one of the maze of paths across the hilly heathland, now, apparently, a good racetrack for the lads on their bikes. I followed my nose. An air shaft pointed me in the right direction, soon to be followed by Tunnel Inn with a charming swinging sign and such street names as Old Portway, Driftwood Close, Pastures Walk and Lime Kiln Close. I was directed to Wast Hills Lane, past the University Farm and on to Tunnel House Cottage, just beyond which was the narrow path through woodland down to the tunnel and the towpath.

The deep cutting after the tunnel kept out most of the autumn sunlight. It kept out noise, too, and the silence and peace were total. For a few minutes I could have been deaf until I emerged in the sunshine and open country and crossed the Birmingham–Redditch road at Hopwood where boats were moored and where the Hopwood House pub by the bridge banned motorcycles, and motorcyclists, too, I expect.

I felt something of an undesirable myself as I scrabbled along the canal 'path', doing my tight-rope trick on the line of bricks supporting the bank, doubling up to avoid being torn to pieces by the overgrowth and trying, at the same time, not to skid into the canal or plop ankle deep in the mud. The trial soon passed and I was rewarded with the lovely view over the Bittell reservoirs to the Lickey Hills and its country park beyond.

The canal skirts the village of Alvechurch. I decided to go through it to see its impressive ancient church, commanding from its hill-top position, and its delightful black and white timbered buildings gathered round the main road to Birmingham. I looked down Bear Hill to the heart of the village which holds on to its old-world charm despite the rush of traffic tearing through. Scarfield Wharf, at the bottom of the village, was almost as busy with moorings for about 150 boats. It was not far to the next tunnel, Shortwood, a mere 562 metres long, and as I started on the path up the hill, I could see the lights of a boat entering from the other end. The path was steep, quite unusual for a canal walk, and when it reached a gate, I was left guessing as to which way to go. My nose, which has picked up an instinct for such things, said left. The damn thing was wrong again. I should have gone straight ahead, then half left to a stile at the edge of a patch of trees which mark the return of the canal to daylight.

The next tunnel, the Tardebigge, with a wharf at each end, is not far away. The path up to the original old wharf is hard-going, and I finished up following the lane at the side as the canal headed into the 530-metre tunnel. Having had my faith in my nose and its instincts severely dented, my trust even wavered in the Public Footpath sign across the road at the end of the lane. But I struck out across the meadow to the top of the hill and the marvellous sight of the slender spire of the eighteenth-century

St Bartholomew's Church and the canal stretching away in the distance towards Worcester.

Now for the Tardebigge flight of locks, thirty of them in about two miles. Some young Americans approaching Lock No. 50, nine from the top, were happy with their time. 'Not bad today,' one drawled. '2½ hours.' From a bridge about halfway down the locks I looked across to nearby Bromsgrove, then back up the hill I was on. There was another good reason for having Worcester as the finishing point: this two miles was all downhill for me!

I had a quick look at a funny old tumbledown barn at Whitford Bridge before taking in the Stoke Prior Locks and lingering at the wharf with its boatyard and warehouses, old canal houses and a pub, the Navigation. A little further on is the site of an old saltworks that must have brought a good deal of trade to the canal. This was the works run by John Corbett, for whom a glass window was placed in the nearby St Michael's Church at Stoke Prior, a tribute to his decision that women and girls should no longer work in his salt pits.

The railway runs with the canal from Stoke Prior past the Astwood flight of five locks with Hanbury, its church and National Trust hall, built in 1701, a mile or more to the left. From Hanbury Wharf ran the Droitwich Junction Canal, running parallel with the old Roman road, the Salt Way into Droitwich where it joined the Droitwich Barge Canal, opened in 1771 and which wandered nearly seven miles to link up with the River Severn at Hawford, a few miles above Worcester. Droitwich is a nice old place, once the site of a Roman camp, a healing and health centre – a spa, that lovely word that suggests gentility, bathchairs, pink gins and oodles of money.

The Worcester and Birmingham Canal goes through Hadzor before reaching its fifth and final tunnel, the Dunhampstead, only 216 metres long. A few scattered buildings with a trim little church close to the water make up Oddingley, soon to be followed by Tibberton before the canal crosses the M5 motorway and takes in the six-flight Offerton Locks before reaching Blackpole and the first sight of Worcester. Industry takes some of the edge off the feeling, but soon the real city of Worcester is reached, starting with the Commandery at the King's Head Lock, the last before Diglis Basin and entry to the Severn. The building, mainly from the fifteenth century, was the headquarters of Charles II

One of the locks on the Tardebigge flight on
the Worcester and Birmingham Canal.

before the battle of Worcester in 1651, and one of the rooms is the King's room because Charles slept there. On the way to Diglis Basin is the Worcester Royal Porcelain factory which used to take coal off the canal to fire its kilns.

Yes, I was glad I had chosen to finish up at Worcester. I love the place. I walked, as I have done so often, on to the banks of the Severn and turned my face to the city. To the cathedral, in particular, the fairest in all England. On the other side of the river is the county cricket ground. The Civil War battle was fought across it, and Charles watched progress from the tower of the cathedral. It was a time of quiet inside the cathedral. And when it is evensong it is a step back through hundreds of years, beyond King Charles's time, perhaps even to King John, whose tomb lies here and whose sculptured effigy is the earliest royal one in this country. I moved beyond King John to Prince Arthur's chantry, the beautiful little chapel to the son of Henry VII, elder brother of Henry VIII, who would have governed England if he had not died at fifteen. Whenever I am in Worcester, I never miss standing in the chantry where kings and queens have stood, where people have been for nearly five hundred years. It is good for perspectives. It is good for the soul. It is a wonderful place to end the day. Amen.

DISTANCE OF WALK: 30 MILES.   **OS MAPS 139 and 150**

12

Wyrley and Essington Canal

Nobody need feel lonely on the Wyrley and Essington Canal. It spends nearly all its fairly short life of about seventeen miles close to people, working and playing with them, peering into their living-rooms and kitchens and workshops. It is regarded as one of the most rural sections of the Birmingham Navigation but you could not really, not in all honesty, class it as one of your true rurals, running through meadow and field, watched for miles only by cows and moorhens. It is a hard-working canal, industrious but friendly and gregarious. It spends a little time in the country but seems more itself when it gets back among houses and factories, running under busy highways, cutting through the town, meeting lots of old friends on the way. Nearly all its bridges are named, with one or two treasures like Devil's Elbow Bridge and the Adam and Eve. I have tried to discover why the Adam and Eve was so named. I asked a young woman nearby. 'Don't know. Nice name though, isn't it?' Another woman unaccountably blushed and blurted: 'Nothing to do with me.'

The Wyrley and Essington is the most northern part of the Birmingham Navigation as it stretches up beyond Brownhills, across the old Watling Street. Wyrley and Essington are two villages in the Black Country, unidentified on many maps, unacknowledged in most books of the area. Yet a canal was named after them, created in 1792 to take coal from the rich mines in and around there. There is Great Wyrley and Little Wyrley but just one Essington, three miles away on the other side of the M6 motorway. The canal took their coal and wandered around the country, gathering in a few more bags from one place and another and throwing out more arms than any Hindu goddess in its search for more goods to transport.

It roams its way to Wolverhampton, rolling about like a drunken man in a fog, so uncertain of its way that it almost catches up with its own tail as it tries to get out of Bloxwich. Yet it has one arm so straight and sure that, as I looked through Friar Bridge, where the Cannock Canal leaves the main line, I swore I could see every other bridge for two miles in its arch. But it is its meanderings that give it its friendliness, touching so much of Black Country life, from its children who skip their way to school on its banks to the old men strolling their way through familiar land.

I joined the canal at its northernmost point, at the end of the old Anglesey branch, which was originally built as a feeder from the Chasewater Reservoir, now a watersports pleasure park. The branch was opened up and made navigable in 1850 to provide transport from Lord Anglesey's mines. It heads quickly for the A5, the great road from London to Holyhead, the old Watling Street, a name that lingers on in the area. The old canal stays with the ancient road for a while, trundling on alongside the fast-moving traffic before turning south to form a natural border for the town of Brownhills, making three parts of a moat as it splits at Catshill with the main line heading up England again, and the Rushall Canal shooting south for Birmingham. It is just above this junction, at Ogley Hays, where the Anglesey used to leave the main line. But the main line is no more. Here it used to take itself off down a long flight of locks towards Lichfield and the Coventry Canal, until it was closed in 1945, leaving the Anglesey section and its connecting reservoir as the top point in the Birmingham Navigation. After the Catshill Junction the canal heads back towards the A5 before a sharp left turn takes it between the supports of an old railway line and under Cooper's Bridge. I just could not place the delightful smell that lingered all round the area, overpowering everything else, until I came across the sheds near the bank and heard the grunting and snuffling of the pigs inside. I hurried – no, rushed – on to Becks Bridge and another right-angled turn past some new housing and, in a garden near the water, several beautiful white doves and a cote.

A good old iron bridge takes the path over the water to the start of the Cannock Canal, opened in 1858 and as straight as a guardsman's arm from Friar Bridge and the stables. 'It goes up to Norton,' an old man told me as he vainly tried to control a young, headstrong red setter. 'Just pleasure boats now, tha knows.' There is a touch of the country here, with Pelsall Wood Common alongside the towpath and the first hint of quiet from traffic and industry. Lord Hay's branch line, a mile away, has not survived time as successfully as the Cannock arm but the route that lasted

Sneyd Junction on the Wyrley and Essington Canal.

from 1800 to 1954 and carried coal from His Lordship's mines to the furnaces of the Black Country is still visible. Another familiar reminder of the past comes at Freeths Bridge, where the towing rope has eaten so deeply into the iron support at the edge of the bridge that the bar resembles a row of teeth.

Everyday life is soon back in force with the houses and high-rise flats of Little Bloxwich, the squeal of children at play-time – how comforting to hear the bell still being used to call them back – and a waterside pub, the Bridgewater: 'Boating enthusiasts welcome.' Industry is not far behind, loudly represented by a copper-refinery where the banging and clattering carry on behind a huge smokescreen which billows across the open common and over the grazing horses, on to the sewage works. Oh, bliss.

The six cooling towers and three chimneys of the power station at Walsall loom large as the canal takes on the appearance of a second-hand shop with doors, oil drums and a mattress sitting on the surface. The M6 motorway throws in its own distinctive noise as the canal makes a sharp V-turn at Sneyd Junction, where a line used to run due north smack between the villages of Wyrley and Essington.

The lock cottage at the start of the abandoned Bentley
Arm of the Wyrley and Essington Canal.

For a time the canal runs with the motorway, first on one side, then the other, before turning its back on it in boredom and heading across country in the general direction of Wolverhampton. An egg-blue car, which had presumably lost its way, was almost totally submerged in the water near Bentley Wharf Bridge – 'The M6 is the other way!' – before housing started to take over the surroundings again with lots of bright new boxes, greenhouses bursting with tomatoes and chrysanths, a good selection of conifers and even a parade of pigeons, dourly studying the water.

Pinfold Bridge took me off the canal and into Wednesfield, chock full of shops and offering an immediate choice of hostelry with the Royal Tiger and the Dog and Partridge, a smartly painted building near where the bull-baiting was held. In fact it is said that the stake was buried only when the land was built up to take the canal. I hurried on, past the Dog and Partridge with its black timbering painted on the whitewashed building.

How I wish I had read Phil Drabble's book on the Black Country before I went to Wednesfield, instead of a few days later. For according to Mr Drabble, anybody who passed the Dog and

Partridge made a big mistake. He described it as 'the one bright spot shining over the canal bridge. . . . Beneath the black and white painted plaster is a genuinely ancient half-timbered building, and only when you get inside do you really appreciate its character. On the left of the little passage door is a tiny bar with a cavernous great fireplace stretching half along the wall. . . . A hospitable great fire polishes the copper and brasses on the mantel-shelf until they glisten in contrast to its blackened age and wink knowingly to show their gratitude. The tables are solid and scrubbed, the floor is of clean red quarries and the glasses shine like crystal. Here is a real old pub which hasn't altered down the years.' Surely, I convinced myself, it must have changed. Hadn't it?

The canal is near its end. The abandoned Bentley Arm – once a busy water connecting with the Walsall Canal – shoots off to the left, past the 'No Through Road' sign, through the weed-ridden locks and tumbling downhill to the chimneys beyond. In about a mile the Wyrley and Essington runs into the main Birmingham line at Wolverhampton's Horseley Fields Junction, fittingly deep in industry. A signpost points to Birmingham to the left, Aldersley to the right, along the Staffordshire and Worcestershire, and back the way I had come to Walsall and Cannock. And the Dog and Partridge at Wednesfield?

DISTANCE OF WALK: 17 MILES.   **OS MAP 139**

13

Ashby Canal

The Battle of Bosworth, one of the most significant events in English history, was fought over land that now takes in part of the Ashby-de-la-Zouch canal in Leicestershire. The battle was fought in 1485, the canal was constructed more than three hundred years later, a mile or two of it running past Bosworth Field and Ambion Wood and near the spot where the victor, Henry VII, put on the crown of England. When the thirty-mile waterway was built in 1805, from the Coventry Canal at Bedworth to Moira below Ashby-de-la-Zouch, the battlefield was somewhere about the middle. The canal served the collieries, and so confident were people that their fortunes were just around the corner that £15,000 was subscribed from Ashby residents alone, among them many tradesmen, including a postilion, peruke-maker, cordwainer, hosiers, bakers and grocers. But it took twenty years for the canal to prosper through an improvement in the coal. Ironically, it was the coal that caused great damage to the canal through subsidence, causing the top nine miles to be abandoned and bringing the terminus down to Snarestone outside the coalfield.

I left the bus close to the canal's junction with the Coventry Canal on the edge of Bedworth and was quickly made to feel at home with a sign from Ashby Canal Association welcoming me to the twenty-one lock-free miles. I was immediately in the middle of the countryside, although still close enough to life to feel the draught of the London express heading towards Rugby fifteen miles away. Florencia glided by. 'It doesn't look very easy walking,' a woman called. It was not. The bank sloped from the hedge, and I seemed forever on the lean, too often into the hedge itself as the path took me close to the water. In the end I bowed to the inevitable, leaving the path through the hedge to resume walking by the side of a wheat field, watching the canal over barbed wire and hedge with one eye, and using the other to keep a watch out for the farmer. It was fifteen minutes before I could return to the towpath, in time to see the church tower of Burton Hastings right behind several large stacks of hay. The farm looked ready for the winter, rather the way we fill the pantry at home in readiness for the next siege.

People on boats usually acknowledge walkers, and I was surprised when I did not get a friendly wave from the people on board a boat called *Ratbag*. It made me wonder if people could take on the character of their boat names the way some folk tend to look like their dogs. The next boat to pass by was *Joli Alfred II*. I did not get a smile out of him either, which quickly blew that theory sky high.

The canal holds on to its remoteness by bypassing Hinckley, a town with a long history of hosiery, and resumes its run through pleasant, rolling farmland to Basin Bridge leading off to Higham on the Hill and where the Waterways Board have listed a selection of 'do nots' including throwing stones and firing guns. I could just make out the words through bullet-ridden holes. I thought I might get a chance to try out again my theory on people and boat names but unfortunately there was nobody aboard *Painted Lady* or *The Vixen*. Just my luck.

The canal is so quiet and for the most part so isolated that I found myself talking to the ducks as I approached Stoke Golding, where the spire of the beautiful medieval church dominates the landscape and which must have been in view for the soldiers at Bosworth. The battlefield is near. There is car-parking at Sutton Cheney Wharf, where a notice announced a medieval joust with falconry and hawking and entertainment from Atherstone Girls' Band and the Barmen of Bosworth. Bosworth is among the best-presented of English battlefields with a battlefield centre and plaques to set the widespread scene. The canal winds round Ambion Wood, where so much of the battle raged, and on between Shenton and Sutton Cheney, where the two sides camped the night before. An aqueduct takes the canal over the Shenton road – an 'acckyduck' as my grandad used to pronounce it. When I was little, I knew exactly where the 'acckyduck' was whenever he referred to it. But what it was remained a mystery for many years.

It was not far to the road to Market Bosworth, a delightful market town a mile away where Doctor Johnson taught at a grammar school founded in Tudor times. It was market day, and the place was all of a bustle, jostling round the stalls in the market place. The canal, meanwhile, continues its quiet, pastoral way to Congerstone, Shackerstone, near where Handel is believed to have composed the *Messiah*, and Snarestone, built over the 250-yard tunnel. The canal ends about half a mile on, a country canal, rustic and private, a satisfying walk after the early, overgrown miles.

DISTANCE OF WALK: 21 MILES.   **OS MAP 140**

14

Erewash Canal

As a boy D. H. Lawrence must have spent many hours on the banks of the Erewash Canal, watching the barges carrying the coal from the pits to the towns. When he was born, in 1885, the canal was already over a hundred years old, running along the edge of his home town, Eastwood, in the heart of the mining area. The Erewash and Nottingham Canals and the River Erewash all ran close together, marvellous playgrounds for young boys who had to make their own amusements in the closing years of the nineteenth century. Whether they were happy hours for David Herbert Lawrence, fourth of five children of a miner, it is hard to say. There was a lot of sadness in his life, even for a bright youngster educated at Nottingham High School and the University College. He became a teacher, but he could so easily have become a miner, like his father, perhaps even working close to the canal.

The Erewash was promoted by Derbyshire and Nottinghamshire colliery-owners to obtain coal from the Erewash valley. Within three years of the public meeting at Heaton in 1776 to hear proposals, the canal was complete, twelve miles of it from the River Trent, near Long Eaton, to Langley Mill, close to Eastwood. It cost only £21,000 to build and was one of the most prosperous in the country, with plenty of trade from collieries, ironworks, brickworks, foundries. Shares which had cost £100 became worth £1,300, and the Derby, Nutbrook and Cromford Canals joined on to add to the prosperity. The Erewash is the only one to survive, a short but delightful stretch of water, totally navigable and easily walkable. I use 'delightful' without any reservations, even though this is largely an industrial area.

The canal starts at Trent Lock, a mile from Long Eaton and a gathering place for the weekend trippers who sample the air and watch the world go by at a busy junction that needs a motorway-type sign to direct the boats. River Trent and the North to the left, the River Soar and the South top left, the Trent and Mersey Canal here, a weir over there. And the Erewash off somewhere else. The lock is the first of fourteen on the Erewash, and the entrance, when I was there last, was thick with the seed of marine growth which had floated to the surface from the bed of the canal. A Waterways Board man was on duty. 'It can get two and three feet thick at times,' he said. 'It can become a problem. We'll get in the boat and push it down to the river with a plank. But it can grow again inside a few hours. It usually comes in the summer. Lasts just a few weeks.'

The Trent is wide here and active with a boat club at its edge, seagoing vessels at the side, anglers on the banks, all watched over by the cooling towers of Ratcliffe Power Station. Alongside the lock is the Steamboat Inn, built in 1791 by the canal company and originally called the Erewash Navigation Inn, and full of sailing mementoes, winches, steering wheels, maps, lamps, pictures, even a mock figurehead. There is an anchor and chain outside, rather bigger than anything needed by the boats passing the front door these days. 'Dead slow past houseboats,' read a notice as I set off for Langley Mill. I obediently slowed to a crawl as I took in the houseboats with tiled tops and shuttered windows.

Two lads were in front of me, one with a Jack Russell terrier, Sally, on a lead. Sally's owner was recounting a day 'on t' Trent wi' t' dog.' 'Red hot it were. Thought I'd throw her in. Let her cool down a bit. But there were too many fishing so I went down to this narrow bit, jutting out. Grass had grown at t' side, making it look wider than what it were. Next I know is she's hanging on th' end o' t' chain, dangling theer, choking away. Thick as a pudding, our Sally.' They laughed. I wondered if D. H. Lawrence had a dog.

I was soon at Long Eaton. Several gardens, with boats at the bottom, run down to the canal where Canada geese often float around, waiting, perhaps, for the remains of somebody's dinner. More marine growth had turned the canal into a green lane. Worshippers were spilling out of the Catholic church of St Francis of Assisi, and on the other side of the water a couple of soccer teams were getting stuck into the new season. Old lace-mills with capped chimneys look down as the canal glides on, past more of the many gardens that make the journey so pleasant. There was colour in the canal, too, with the white of the lilies contrasting

Erewash Canal at Long Eaton.

with the green of the marine growth. I drifted on to Sandiacre lock, driving eight cows off the path as I went. If I had looked more closely, I probably would not have bothered. They were bulls.

Here is the junction with the old Derby Canal, fourteen miles long, which linked with the Trent and Mersey at Swarkestone, an upturned Y of a canal with Derby at the end. What a pity it is still not in existence for it had an unusual piece of towpath that would have been worth the lengthy detour. The canal crossed the River Derwent on the level just upstream of a semi-circular weir. The towpath was a narrow timber bridge about three hundred feet long and known as the Long Horse-bridge. It shielded narrow-boats from being swept over the weir in times of flood but was often damaged by debris. Pedestrians could use the bridge, which was demolished in 1959, but not with 'wheel perambulators or barrows that may impede the passage of horses'.

A notice near the Red Lion at Sandiacre declared that on the following day – a Bank Holiday Monday – there would be a tug o' war between the girls and boys – across the canal! A little further along, the pretty Sandiacre parish church, standing on a rise known as Stoney Clouds and considered locally as 'the last of the Pennines', makes the perfect picture with a farm at its feet. It is a lovely scene, being succeeded by the less compelling sight of a tangle of railway lines, so many I thought I might have wandered off to Crewe. The M1 motorway is nearby, too, but once under it the canal takes off into the country, past the derelict Stanton Ironworks.

Trowell church tower is to the right, bobbing about behind the hawthorns, the textile town of Ilkeston lies ahead, and somewhere near, playing hide and seek and staying fairly well hidden, is the River Erewash. Two cricket matches were being conducted in a perfect setting with the church as a backcloth. The ancient hilltop town of Ilkeston has an eight-hundred-year-old parish church and a seven-hundred-year-old annual Town Fair which goes on for three days. I did read that the fair starts on the first Thursday after the first Sunday after 11 October. Which could put it around Christmas time, I suppose. Let's just call it the Autumn Fair.

The canal passes more gardens, on beyond Stenson Lock – named after a local family – and through the columns of the viaduct that once carried the Great Northern Railway over the canal, the neighbouring river and the derelict Nottingham Canal. Two men, splendid in blazers and ties, walked by. 'You get barges on here,' said one. 'Nice holiday, barging.' 'I don't know,' said the other. 'Makes me sick.'

Mining subsidence has caused the bridge to slip and the wall to crack at Cotmanhay, and one or two boats can have problems getting through. There are no such problems for the foot-sloggers, who are rewarded with a splendid view, a church and chimney at Eastwood, the hills rising to the right with houses at Awsworth, and lingering history at Shipley Wharf. Shipley Boat Inn stands a hundred yards from the lock, rather grand for an inn with several bars and a restaurant, and close by, alongside the path, are two buildings, one of which was a slaughter house for injured pit ponies and old canal horses. The canal and river change sides near the Shipley Boat Inn, where the line of the old railway is still marked by the stone bases for the bridges, one of them deep in water. Heanor church slips by on the hill to the left before the canal meets its end in the Great Northern Basin at Langley Mill where there is a welcome from the Erewash Canal Preservation and Development Association. A man, thin-faced and bearded, wearing a brown tweed suit with breeches, smiled pensively as he went by, heading for Eastwood. I must have been day-dreaming. I thought for a minute I was back at the turn of the century.

DISTANCE OF WALK: 12 MILES.   **OS MAP 129**

15

Grand Union Canal

On page 22 the southern section of this great canal was described. Here now are three of its Midlands sections.

Market Harborough to Leicester

I do not need much of an excuse to go to Market Harborough. The old market town has a charm and a winning smile that are irresistible. I like its broad main street, the fish restaurant and the Red Cow, the market place itself, the timbered grammar school on legs. There is a good feel about the place. It must be its age, a solid piece of England, small but secure, a reminder of our history, with an eight-hundred-year-old market, a medieval church, stage-coach inns and a school getting on for four hundred years old. The Three Swans is the best of the coaching inns, with a large wrought-iron sign that is regarded as one of the finest in the country. I enjoy walking off the main street, through the narrow entrance into its courtyard, past the stables to the back entrance. Market Harborough stands on the A6 road and was on the stage-coach route to London from Nottingham and Sheffield.

According to the sign, it is only fourteen miles from Market Harborough to Leicester. By canal, though, it is more than half as long again. About twenty-three miles. The start, from the Market Harborough Basin, just off the A6 Leicester road, is deceptive, lulling the unwary into a false sense of security. The first move is in roughly the right direction before two sharp loops take it twice across the A6 before finally heading off towards Foxton and the main line of the canal. The sound of traffic is soon left far behind as the canal explores for hours the fine Leicestershire countryside with its variety of fields. A powerful-looking Friesian bull froze me with a glare from across the water; two men with rifles climbed into a nearby field as a bi-plane buzzed and bumped overhead. A butterfly flirted with me, floating from flower to flower, keeping just a move ahead all the time. Its delicacy

Foxton, on the Market Harborough branch of
the Grand Union Canal.

contrasted with the vigorous wriggle of a tail into the hedge. A
snake perhaps. Smoke drifted across the canal from burning
stubble. In the field next to me was hay, rolled up like a bandage,
all ready to be wheeled to the barn.

The junction with the main Leicestershire line of the canal was
thick with people wandering around the flight of ten locks that is
as straight as a stair, and hunting for signs of the lift that was used
at the start of the century. The system was to float boats in two
water-tanks which ran on rails up and down the hill, greatly
reducing the operation time. The lift worked on steam which had
to be kept available all the time and which became uneconomical,
forcing its closure after only eleven years. There is not much of it
left. People scrambled about the hillside, through the undergrowth, looking for signs. The foundations of the engine room
and the cut that took craft to the bottom of the plane are still there.
Foxton Inclined Plane Trust was working hard in its campaign for
restoration. 'Buy a brick for £1.'

The Foxton flight of locks on the Grand Union Canal.

It was five minutes past opening time and the pub's garden at the side of the water was already full. Inside were interesting old pictures of local scenes; outside the Vagabond Cruise boat hooted itself hoarse as it prepared for its 12.40 trip. I walked alongside the boat with its sixteen passengers for fifteen minutes, then it turned round, leaving me alone again with sixteen miles to go and hardly a village along the way. The lovely village of Gumley, Saddington, with its seven-hundred-year-old church, Fleckney and Kilby slipped by on the left, Smeeton Weston and Kibworth Beauchamp on the right. Between came Debworth Wharf and Sniddington Tunnel, the wharf with barges that looked to be hiding and farmers loading hay under cover as a threatening storm drew near. The storm had decided to settle elsewhere by the time I reached the tunnel, half a mile long and said to be haunted by a headless woman who had been decapitated in the tunnel. There is no towpath but, even if there had been and even if the storm had unleashed its wrath on me, I do not think I would have set foot inside that tunnel.

I followed the path over the hill, on to a lane with a hedge either side, and more hay, stacked in fields like a thousand swiss rolls. A sign was riddled with gunshot but I could just make it out: 'British Railways. Grand Junction Canal, Leicester Branch'. The canal is soon among the Kibworth Locks, the start of the long forty-lock downhill run to the River Trent thirty-eight miles away. It was so quiet. No boats, no people, little life. I listened hard for sound and heard the distant murmur of a tractor. It was good to see Wistow church across the fields, dedicated to Wistan, the Christian prince of the Saxon kingdom of Mercia who is said to have been murdered where the church is standing. Just behind stands Wistow Hall, where King Charles I stayed before the Battle of Naseby in 1645. A lane links Wistow with the village of Newton Harcourt, right by the canal with a tiny thirteenth-century church and a manor house from the seventeenth century. I left the canal for a few minutes to savour this quiet old corner of the country on the fringe of Leicester.

The first real housing since Market Harborough, sixteen miles back, arrived with South Wigston, where a man sat in the weed-filled garden of a new house, contentedly fishing. The fields were going. The city was coming. The houses were arriving, some grand with balconies and patios and white metal chairs and tables. The River Sence, which has been around for seven miles, runs into the Soar, and for a time the towpath runs between the two waters. Up to the iron parish boundary marker of 1891 from the parish of Lubbesthorpe into the borough of Leicester, on to the Pack Horse Bridge which crosses the Soar. King Charles is believed to have crossed the bridge on his flight from Naseby.

As Leicester approaches, the canal widens into an enormously broad weir at the joining with the Soar, a strange-looking area where boats are warned to keep in the navigable channel close to the towpath. Leicester has arrived. The church bells were ringing as I walked into the city, up to the West Bridge along a wide, straight, impressive tree-lined stretch.

DISTANCE OF WALK: 23 MILES.   **OS MAPS 140 and 141**

Northampton Arm

Somehow, I just cannot get used to Northampton. I am sure it is a lovely town. It is ancient and attractive. Several delightful-sounding streets reflect its age: Sheep Street, Fish Street, Woolmonger Street, Mercer's Row, The Drapery, Horsemarket, Horseshoe Street, Marefair. It has a grand market place, one of the biggest in England, spacious and rather special. And it has long been popular. Daniel Defoe talked in the 1720s about its beauty: 'the handsomest and best built town in this part of England'. The Reverend William MacRitchie, minister of the parish of Clunie in Perthshire, referred to 'one of the first market places with the best houses and streets of any town in England'. But that was nearly two hundred years ago. They did not go round and round on the one-way system, losing direction and temper. It can warp a man's view of a place. It is so much better to get about by foot, out of the centre, down to the bottom of the town where run the River Nene and the Northampton Arm of the Grand Union Canal.

The river probably means rather more than the canal to the people of Northampton. It enhances Becket Park, named after the Archbishop who was tried and condemned here in the twelfth century, and runs ninety miles to the Wash. The arm of the Grand Union goes off in the other direction, a delightful five-mile run to its mother near the dreamy village of Milton Malsor with its fourteenth-century church, old houses, thatched roofs and tidy gardens. Becket Park was an ideal place to start. Barges added splashes of colour, the breeze ruffled the trees, and as I walked by the river towards the canal a wedding party passed by. On the other side of the river was an Avon works with a gleaming silver chimney that looked as if it was scrubbed every day. A timber yard, a corn merchant's wharf and a three-arched bridge lead to a Carlsberg depot. To get to the canal involves walking away from the river and down Old Towcester Road to meet up with the first of the seventeen locks that take the canal uphill to the main line. The stark 'No Mooring' and 'Keep Out. Private' signs reminded me of one I had seen that summer at a newspaper stall at Marble Arch in London: 'No directions given.' You do not see many more miserable notices than that.

There is the usual cluster of industrial sites to get through before reaching the country – Cotton End Wharf, the nearby Carlsberg, with its high, black finger of a chimney, railway, factories. Head-high weeds tried to hide the water from view but nothing could conceal the sight of Kislingbury with its church spire on the hill three miles ahead.

A new road bridge, standing on huge, concrete drums like cotton bales, runs over the canal which hugs the side of a field so recently swaled that the smell of the burnt chaff was still strong. The evening was well underway. The clouds had hurried off to the horizon, and the sun, low to the right, was shining brightly out of the water. A narrow humped bridge, taking traffic from Rothersthorpe to Hardingstone, forced car-drivers to blow their horns as they neared. I tried identifying cars, at least by size, by the sound of their voices, working upwards from the bleep and burp of the smallest to the blast of the limousines. A monstrosity of a tunnel, about sixty yards long with supporting crossbeams, takes the canal under the M1 motorway and to the first of twelve locks, close together and with an 1882 datemark. The flight makes a good uphill climb through rural countryside near Milton Malsor and into the final mile to the junction where a Grand Junction Canal Company sign gives the mileage to Braunston, 16¾, and Northampton, 5.

DISTANCE OF WALK: 5 MILES.　　　　　　　　**OS MAP 152**

Grand Union Canal near Rowington.

Warwick to Solihull

The main line of the Grand Union is near the end in this fifteen-mile stretch from the enchanting old town of Warwick to Solihull on the edge of Birmingham. The River Avon flows close to Warwick Castle, one of the most famous and best-preserved castles in the country, but the canal keeps to the top end of the town after leaving Leamington Spa and heads for the impressive, dramatic Hatton flight of twenty-one locks. The canal and railway keep company past Hatton Station up to Shrewley Tunnel, a quarter of a mile long and without a towpath. The horsepath over the top, which has its own forty-yard tunnel, goes across the village's main street. The canal wanders on its quiet way, and in parts the towpath looks as if it rarely experiences a walker. It passes close to Rowington, a village associated with four William Shakespeares, all said to be related to the poet, and with a beautiful canalside pub with an endearing name, Tom o' The

The Navigation Inn at Kingswood on
the Grand Union Canal.

Wood. The Navigation Inn at Kingswood looked to be a popular
pub with the anglers, who had left their baskets and rods and
paraphernalia at the door. Here is a connection with the Stratford-upon-Avon Canal in the middle of a heavily locked section,
the Lapworth Locks. The Grand Union keeps to the country for a
while as if fighting off the ever-nearing city of Birmingham, and
takes in another flight of locks at Knowle. It passes under the M42
motorway before reaching the village of Catherine de Barnes and
its popular Boat Inn, a perfect watering hole before the canal
circles Solihull and enters its last few miles to Birmingham.

DISTANCE OF WALK: 15 MILES.   **OS MAPS 139 and 151**

The North

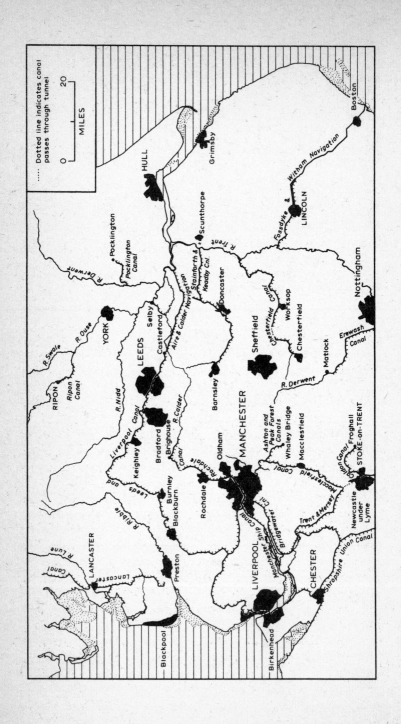

16

Caldon Canal

When L. T. C. Rolt sailed through the Potteries in 1939, it was to the accompaniment of steam, smoke and flame, coke ovens, blast furnaces and canyons of slag. Workmen's faces were streaked with sweat and grime. Today, however, so much of what he experienced has gone. The factories still overpower, but the forest of chimneys has thinned, the fire has gone out of the Potteries' belly.

'The men of North Staffordshire are proud of their smoky sky, for to them it is the symbol of prosperity, and local stationers display picture postcards of typical "smokescapes" for the benefit of rare visitors,' wrote Mr Rolt. 'Though trade was said to be slack, there appeared to our eyes, fresh from the country, to be enough smoke in the air to please the most pessimistic potter, as we approached Etruria summit lock and the junction of the canal to Leek and Froghall, yet another branch of the "Grand Trunk".'

This was the start of the Caldon Canal, climbing its way out of the Potteries, seventeen miles from Etruria and Hanley to Froghall through some extremely beautiful and unspoilt country-side. The Caldon, a branch of the main Trent and Mersey Canal, was opened in 1778 to draw limestone from the quarries of Caldon Low, over three miles beyond Froghall. A system of horse-drawn tramways connected the quarry with the canal terminus, a link that existed until 1920 when the cable incline to Froghall was closed.

Froghall is the beautiful end, deep in the Churnet Valley. A large picnic area surrounds the canal terminus where two barges, watched over by three large, attentive dogs, breathed their smoke into the morning mist. Between 1811 and 1846 the canal had an extension to Uttoxeter, an extra thirteen miles which is still recorded on the mileposts, some of which have only recently been replaced. 'Etruria 17 miles, Uttoxeter 13 miles,' says the first iron post which was put up in May 1983 to replace an original from over 160 years ago. A copper-works runs alongside the towpath but it and its chimney soon fall behind as the canal, with the River Churnet rippling below, runs on through Cherry Eye Bridge, with an unusual Gothic arch, and buries itself in secluded woodland. The Forestry Commission has added to the amenities with a landing stage in Ruelow Wood, providing another picnic place and walk. The surroundings are magnificent, and within three miles the canal reaches Consall Forge, now tranquil and so isolated that a pub, the Black Lion, is not reached by any public road, but where a great, water-powered ironworks once existed. Here the river and the canal join up to become one waterway for the next mile, a beautiful place, a wooded valley up to Oak-meadow Ford Lock where the waters split again and the path runs between them on a narrow limb of land. However secluded the area might have seemed, it did not stop one boat-owner near Willow Cottage worrying about thieves. A sign in his boat window read: 'Please note before stealing engine, address is engraved in casting.'

At times the river is as close as the canal to the towpath, and after being together for seven miles from Froghall, the two split on the far side of Cheddleton, a charming hilltop village with an ancient church and flint-mills with restored waterwheels. The village is up Hollow Lane, high in the sky, fortified by the pub and the church of St Edward the Confessor, dating back to the twelfth century and with commanding views over the Stafford-shire countryside. Hollow Lane was the scene of great excitement when I was there, with two men and a woman in slippers trying desperately to outwit and corner a rather clever guinea fowl. The flint-mills, standing next to the canal, have been opened to the public since 1969, with two splendid waterwheels the centrepiece of attraction. The South Mill was originally a corn-mill from the thirteenth century, and as well as mills and wheels and lots of old stones there are flint kilns, a slip drying kiln and the miller's cottage.

It was a perfect morning in a wonderful setting, the sort of day you might have hand-picked, the sort that makes you greet everybody in sight: 'Lovely morning!' A small man with two dogs kept me company for ten minutes, speaking through lips that gripped a cigarette which was never removed from his mouth. 'Ay, grand as owt,' he enthused, shaking the ash on to the ground. He had developed to a fine degree the art of smoking

One of the waterwheels at Cheddleton Flint Mills
on the Caldon Canal.

without using his hands, which were stuffed deep in his trouser
pockets. He kept a careful watch as the cigarette burned nearer
and nearer to his mouth, puckering his lips and squinting from
time to time, judging the remains to a nicety before spitting them
out. Clever as owt . . .

Across the fields and up against the hill I could see the tops of
the boats on the Leek branch. As the two canals closed in on one
another, I bridged the gap up the road towards Longsdon,
joining the 2½-mile-long Leek branch near where a mother and
son were drinking from the canal. Cows, of course. Here is more
relaxing scenery, a wooded stretch with attractive houses and
long, sloping gardens to the water, including a rock garden with
an impressive selection of heathers. The 130-yard tunnel was
closed – 'Danger. Keep Out' – but the horse-path over the hill was
open for business as usual, leading to a view of Leek golf course
with the smart club house and downhill fairway. Leek itself
opens out through the last bridge with the cemetery in the
background and a car-breaker's at the front. The canal runs out of
water on an aqueduct over the Churnet on the edge of town, up
against wire fencing and a few thousand concrete pipes. The
return journey was past Stillwater Cottage and along an impressive embankment that carries the branch over the railway, Endon
Brook and the main line of the canal. A sharp turn right puts the
Leek branch parallel with, but twenty-four feet above, the Caldon
Canal for half a mile until they join at Hazlehurst, where three
locks carry the main line up to the level of the branch which is
crossed by an 1842 iron bridge.

Endon appears on the right before another footbridge takes the
path over the short arm used by the Stoke-on-Trent Boat Club for
moorings. Just beyond is the strange sight of a large iron wheel in
the middle of the canal, all that remains of a bridge on which light
engines from a connecting railway pivoted. Stockton Brook Locks
start to carry the canal on its run down to Stoke-on-Trent and the
Potteries, and at Engine Lock, named after a steam-powered
engine that pumped water from a nearby mine, the country is all
behind. The factories come up fast, and one of them, at Milton, is
still using the waterway to transport pottery goods to and from
another factory three miles away at Hanley.

The River Trent, still in its infancy in these parts, runs below for
a time as the canal, now looking untidy and forlorn, goes through

The Leek branch of the Caldon Canal.

wasteland and housing which gathers in on the edge of Hanley. The buildings are coming closer, tannoy announcements in adjoining works echo on all sides, high-rise flats stay in sight for too long, and a huge, derelict factory emphasizes the sense of emptiness that is so engulfing. The scene brightens as the canal goes through Hanley Park, close to its end, where the first glimpse of the Trent and Mersey fittingly appears between factories on the left. The Caldon drops through two staircase locks and five minutes later is at the junction with the Trent and Mersey, a meeting no longer heralded with steam and flame and smokescapes. Mr Rolt might have been disappointed at the shortage of dramatic effects, but nothing could deny that for three-quarters of its length the Caldon Canal is absolutely lovely. As grand as owt.

DISTANCE OF WALK: 17 MILES.
(LEEK BRANCH 2½ MILES). OS MAP 162

17

Macclesfield Canal

There were a few things I wanted to see on the Macclesfield Canal: the telescope at Jodrell Bank, that great hill with the lovely sounding name, the Cloud, the monument called White Nancy near Bollington, Mow Cop with its folly, the Bird in Hand pub where I understood the beer was still brought up in a jug from the cellar – and Lovers' Leap, where a couple had committed suicide by jumping into the canal, their wrists tied together.

I had read that the bridge at Whiteley Green bore the inscription 'Lovers' Leap 1891'. I wandered round, on the Bollington side, then on the Marple side, on the road above and the towing path beneath, but I could not see it. I tried again, more carefully this time, feeling each stone as I went. Then I found it, the engraving with small letters that were gradually fading with time. In the middle of the top stone on the Marple side of the bridge were the words: 'Lovers' Leap June . . .'. Either 1891 or 1894. The story was that a young couple had drowned themselves because their hopes of marriage were being thwarted by their parents. The nearby inn, the Windmill, was said to be haunted – by the ghosts of the unlucky lovers. The real story proved a little different.

The bodies of Walter Brindley, who was twenty-five, and Esther Pickford, aged twenty-nine, were discovered in the canal near Whiteley Green Bridge on Friday 22 June 1894. At the inquest the following week it was said that the two people were joined together by a handkerchief tied together at the wrists. They had been in the water a day or two. The report in the *Macclesfield Courier and Herald* said a boat had turned up the bodies in the Manchester, Sheffield and Lincolnshire Railway Company's canal at Whiteley Green, Adlington.

Brindley, a journeyman baker and married, and Pickford, a single woman, both worked for the baker, Joseph France, in Park Lane, Macclesfield. They were seen together on Sunday afternoon near Butley, not far from Whiteley Green, and Brindley's

Factory on the bank of the Macclesfield Canal near Bollington.

wife got to hear about it. When he got home, he turned out his wife and took in his companion on the Tuesday. This enraged neighbours 'and a mêlée ensued', with windows being broken, curtains burned and blinds pulled down. The disturbance was renewed the following morning, and police had to find shelter for the woman. The couple were seen for the last time that evening in the neighbourhood of Bollington. Brindley's widow was left with three children. And the Windmill Inn? Well . . . the bodies were taken from the canal to the inn that Friday lunchtime. The pub is still there, but it was just too late to sample their beer . . .

The Macclesfield Canal, which shares with the Peak Forest the distinction of being the highest navigation in the country at around five hundred feet above sea level, is twenty-eight miles long and almost entirely rural. A lovely walk through relaxing country and high enough to look down on fields and trees, and a few rooftops. It leaves the Trent and Mersey Canal by the Canal Tavern at Hardings Wood, near Kidsgrove railway station in the Potteries, starting life through the bridge that bears its name with the date 1829 in Roman numerals. A three-way signpost for Middlewich, Stoke and Marple stands at the junction.

The canal was opened to traffic from Hardings Wood to Marple, where it linked with the Peak Forest, in 1831, one of the last waterways to be built and well after the peak period for canal building. But it was the last link in the chain from Manchester through the Potteries and the Midlands to the south of England, its main cargoes being coal and cotton.

After leaving the Trent and Mersey, the Macclesfield runs alongside it for half a mile before taking a sharp turn right to fly over it near lock 42. The canal reaches the stop lock at Hall Green within a mile, a nuisance of a lock with a rise of only a foot, a continuing relic of the petty jealousies which existed in the days of canal construction. For the stop lock was designed purely to make sure that the Macclesfield Canal did not get any of the Trent and Mersey's water. At the same time the clever old Trent and Mersey had the right to take all the water coming down the Macclesfield Canal!

Mow Cop soon emerges, one of Cheshire's landmarks, over a thousand feet high with artificial ruins on its summit, erected at the end of the eighteenth century by Randle Wilbraham who lived about three miles away at Rode on the towpath side of the

One of the lovely roving bridges on the Macclesfield Canal.

canal. Almost in the shadow of Mow Cop is the lovely little pub, the Bird in Hand, right next to the swing bridge at Kent's Green. A small double-fronted cottage, really, with a tiny bay window, the Smoke Room.

My first milestone, four feet high with a curved gravestone top, told me I was four miles from Hall Green, the original terminus, and twenty-five from Marple, rather longer than the true distance. Not far away is the eighteenth-century red-bricked Ramsdell Hall, presenting its wide front to the canal, and the spire of the fourteenth-century church at Astbury, just too far away to visit. I wish I had had time to go, if only to see the yew tree that was said to be ancient when King Edward III, in the fourteenth century, made it compulsory to plant yew trees in churchyards to provide bows for the longbowmen. The canal also manages to miss Congleton, a market and silk-manufacturing town with some fine Georgian houses, as it runs away to the east under two lovely roving bridges, designed so the horse could follow the towpath to the other bank without being unhitched.

Cobbles lead out of the squelchy path to where a footbridge used to pass over the canal's overflow. Now just the stone bases stand across the channel which guides the water into a tumbling stream down to Shaw Brook, snaking its way under the railway viaduct in the valley. And was that hill I could see really the Cloud, the Bosley Cloud? A woman in a canalside garden at Buglawton mildly chided me for referring to the hill. 'The Cloud is a mountain. It's a lovely walk to the top, and you can see across to Wales and Lancashire. Ever so nice.' I should have asked, too, about Havannah, a mile away, a village built in the middle of the eighteenth century around a silk mill and its name originating in the capture of the capital of Cuba.

The canal wanders on through peaceful green country before crossing the railway for the third time in two miles. The London train was whistling over the twenty-arched viaduct over the Dane, which is also crossed by the canal before it enters the Bosley Locks, the only ones on the canal apart from the stop lock at Hall Green. A Waterways Board man identified the Telecom tower on Sutton Common and promised me a sight of Jodrel! Bank from the top lock. The tower had taken over from the Cloud, brooding above the flight of twelve locks which lifts the canal 110 feet in just over a mile. But still I could not see Jodrell Bank. Still no sign of the telescope.

A walk that is largely through fields, past farms and hills, turns to woodland for a while, a lovely tree-lined section towards the Fool's Nook. The pub has changed its name but the swivel bridge across the road is, happily, still the Royal Oak Bridge, and I sat alongside it, to be quickly joined by a man in shiny black breeches, snazzy black stockings, vivid red anorak and red-and-white peaked cap. A cyclist. 'Jodrell Bank? Yes, you'll see it if you go up there,' he said, pointing to the towering Gawsworth Common. He knew something about the Cloud as well. 'My dad used to say if there was a cloud on it, it would rain.'

The silk town that gives its name to the canal is approaching, but again it is off to the edges, up the town, over Sutton Brook and looking down on the tiles of the Old King's Head. The tiny snug bar and the roaring open fire were too good to miss, and it took a good deal of willpower to climb back up the embankment to the towpath. Macclesfield stretched out below, and while I might not have been looking down on the church towers, I certainly felt to be looking them in the eye.

As the canal moved on to Bollington, over the aqueduct sixty feet above the road, I looked up at White Nancy, the summer-house at the end of Kerridge Hill, a whitewashed landmark that can be seen for miles. Everybody I asked about its origins had a different story to tell, including Waterloo and the Boer War and connections with the Royal Navy. A jolly, ruddy-faced man who was wrestling with a troublesome tree root at the bottom of his garden, suggested it had something to with Ingersley Hall. 'Down the valley, wealthy family, nobility they were. Stuck it up there. When Lord Haw-Haw was broadcasting from Germany during the war, he said the Germans would come to Manchester and paint White Nancy green. They never did. Now the lads do it for a lark and the council has to whitewash it again.'

The canal moves on towards its end through quiet isolated country, past Lovers' Leap to Higher Poynton and High Lane and into Marple past the massive Goyt Mill. Two more roving bridges finish it off, the first next to the Ring o' Bells Inn, the second to join up with the Peak Forest canal. It is a walk of great charm with a good towpath and plenty to see. But where was Jodrell Bank?

DISTANCE OF WALK: 28 MILES.   **OS MAP 109 and 118**

18

Ashton and Peak Forest Canals

Like a plant that springs to beautiful life after looking dead in the middle of a hard winter, the Ashton and Peak Forest Canals surprisingly blossom into full flower after the most lifeless of starts. Between Manchester and Marple, from city to country, the waterway grows into an object of beauty and splendour. Having walked the twenty-two miles in both directions, I know there is only one way to go, from Greater Manchester to Cheshire and Derbyshire, from darkness into light.

The Ashton is one of four navigable canals with beginnings in the heart of Manchester. The Bridgewater and Ship Canals run south-west to Runcorn and Eastham; the Rochdale, with admittedly less than two miles in the city fit for boats, takes off for the Pennines, while the Ashton heads east. Its beginnings are close to Piccadilly Station in the shadow of mills, office blocks and warehouses, born out of the side of the Rochdale Canal and running through Ancoats, Droylsden and Dukinfield. The Ashton and Peak Forest were constructed separately, the Ashton being completed in 1799, the Peak Forest a year later, except for the Marple flight of locks which was added in 1804.

The Ashton, only six miles long to its link with the Peak Forest at Dukinfield, was a mess of a canal at its start, deep in rubbish as it headed through Ancoats, quickly climbing through the first three of its eighteen locks as it looked for cleaner air. Clothes were hanging on barbed wire near a caravan on wasteland; a hooter called the workers to duty in one of the seemingly unending line of factories, with their fire escapes and escaping steam, that line the banks. The climb continues through locks at Beswick and Clayton, where a bridge leads over the start of the old five-mile branch to Stockport. A glance behind from the top of the Clayton flight shows Manchester spread out below, a more attractive picture at night with its thousands of twinkling lights.

The last two locks on the Ashton are at Fairfield, a pleasant area with its 1833 narrow, stone, packet boat-house, the lock cottage

Dukinfield Junction where the Ashton and Peak Forest Canals meet.

with smoke puffing gently from the chimney, the stone foot-bridge and the branch that once linked Hollinwood. The industrial oppression is passing – or at least taking on a new look and aroma with Robertson's marmalade factory. Portland basin is a picture, tidy and looking cared-for. Signposts point to Stalybridge via Huddersfield Narrow Canal 2¼ miles, Manchester via Droylsden 6 miles, and Marple via Woodley 7¾ miles. The Ashton runs on a little further to join up with the derelict Huddersfield Narrow Canal, leaving the Peak Forest to go off at right angles under a handsome 1835 bridge. The route to Marple is due south across the River Tame, a claimant to be the source of the Mersey. Here is the Peak Forest Canal with its promise of cleaner, healthier, more beautiful things to come. But first, more industry, more signs of man. Once over the Tame, the canal runs under an 1845 iron railway bridge, newly supported in 1978, between Denton and Hyde, through the seventy-five-yard tunnel where the canal has been re-directed to accommodate the M67 motorway and past a poor old mill, cut off at the knees by demolition men but still managing to show its girder with the date 1869. A three-storey 1828 warehouse is followed by the huge red-brick mill of Gee X and the narrow 176-yard Woodley tunnel, cobbled, flagged, puddled, with a wooden hand-rail and a bulging roof.

The canal enters its loveliest stretch around Marple, first passing Romiley and Bredbury Green before running through the second tunnel, the Hyde Bank, over three hundred yards long. The River Goyt, another starter to the Mersey, tumbles and rushes about below as the canal continues on its sedate way through a narrow, buttressed cutting that was once the Rose Hill tunnel, opened out early in the canal's life and left with a rocky surround. The cutting leads on to the mightily impressive Marple Aqueduct with its pink-stone bases and mellowed brown arches a hundred feet over the Goyt. It is a dizzy look down into the wooded valley but at least the towpath side of the twenty-foot-wide aqueduct has a stone parapet. There is no wall, no fence, no protection on the other side, with mooring rings a foot from the edge! And to add to the spectacle, the railway viaduct, built some years later and forty feet higher, stands nearby.

The path moves into woodland and the start of the flight of Marple locks. It is hard work for people on boats, but for the walker it is lovely, even going uphill, past gardens and bridges and folk's front rooms. Just after crossing Station Road, half-way up the hill of locks is the grand warehouse of Samuel Oldknow, where boats were loaded under cover. Mr Oldknow was a benevolent employer with widespread interests. A nearby road was named after him, and even Posset Bridge, where Stockport Road crosses the canal four locks from the top, owes its name to him. It seems he promised the workmen a posset of ale, a drink of hot milk curdled with ale and perhaps flavoured with spices, if they completed the work on time. Presumably they did. Under the road are two separate tunnels, one narrow and oval for the horses, and a similar passage with steps up to the lock for the boatmen. A plaque commemorating the canal's re-opening to navigation in 1974 stands at the head of the flight where the

Warehouse on the Peak Forest Canal.

Macclesfield Canal takes off to the right for Kidsgrove in the Potteries. Across the top basin stands the house that was Jinks's boatyard. The sunken garden was a dry dock standing at the end of an arm that led to Mr Oldknow's lime kilns.

The third section of the Ashton and Peak Forest Canals, the last 6½ miles to Whaley Bridge, has a touch of grandeur about it, riding high on the hillside overlooking the Goyt Valley. The views are extensive, like looking down on Trumpton at times. There is the toy railway, and if you look carefully, you will see the men working in the mill, and look – there is Mrs Rumbleweed, off to the butcher's with her dog, Patch. There is Strawberry Hill and Mellor Moor, Brook Bottom, Lower Cliffe and Windybottom Wood, the river, canal, road and railways, and a host of tempting lanes and footpaths, one with a 'thru route' to Mellor and Cown Edge, another to Hazel Grove – 'Turn right at swing bridge.'

Once past Disley, the canal moves into its third county, Derbyshire, with the spread of New Mills on the other side of the valley. The mixture of scattered industry and wild countryside is a happy blend in this land of great open spaces, and the variety is completed with a sweets factory next to the towpath, with swizzels, fizzers, refreshers, lollipops, double dips and fruity pops.

A mile on and the canal passes the attractive little village of Furness Vale with the path on a level with the bedroom windows of a row of terraced houses. The branch off to Buxworth is only half a mile long, down to the basin which today is classified as an ancient monument after years of busy yesterdays when it was a large inland port. The arm was built to carry the limestone from Dove Holes four miles away in the hills and which had to be carried to the canal basin in small trucks over a tramway. The limestone was processed in the kilns at Buxworth before it was carried away. The basin, disused for more than fifty years, was under restoration when I was last there.

The end of the canal, at Whaley Bridge, is not far from the turn-off for Buxworth. The charming small town is a lovely place to finish a walk, with its old marine buildings, the water running under the centre of one where goods used to be loaded and unloaded under cover between barge and railway wagon.

DISTANCE OF WALK: 22 MILES.   **OS MAPS 109 and 110**

Boats, one of them half submerged, at Waterloo
Bridge at Runcorn, the end of the Bridgewater Canal.

19

Bridgewater Canal

I wonder if I should have walked the Bridgewater the other way round, starting in Manchester instead of Runcorn. Then I could have seen the River Mersey change from being a mere lad near Old Trafford to the giant it becomes near Liverpool. But then I would have missed that wonderful first sight of the river from Runcorn Bridge, an exciting view over the Mersey from high above the rooftops. No, I was right. That is the way to approach the Bridgewater Canal which used to lock into the river there.

It was not much after half past six. Dawn was just breaking, heightening the life and drama of the scene. The cooling towers of the power station at Widnes just across the river were belching their smoke into the cold morning air. A fawn wisp from a tall, thin concrete chimney reached through the yellow dawn for the river which narrows and squeezes through the bridge but which is still impressively wide all about, its mud banks standing high in the shallow water, huge black dots set in sparkling patches of water. The church by the water on the west bank at Widnes peered through the mist and across the river to All Saints, the parish church of Runcorn, and as I walked over the bridge, almost stepping on the tiles of the houses below, I looked down on the Manchester Ship Canal, separated from the river by a concrete pier.

There is no need to look too hard for the Bridgewater. The road swings over it, within sight of its end, up against Waterloo Bridge near the spot where the canal used to jump down to the Mersey through ten locks, now abandoned and filled in, cast off in 1966. Bridgewater Street and Egerton Street are nearby, named after Francis Egerton, the Duke of Bridgewater, whose waterway was the forerunner of modern canals. When he found the Mersey and Irwell Navigation were charging too much for transporting coal from his Worsley collieries to nearby Manchester, he decided to build his own canal. The line to Stretford was opened in 1765, the extension to Runcorn eleven years later.

Old Runcorn is to be found by the docks. From the attractive black and white iron bridge where the Bridgewater now meets its Waterloo and where boats moor right up to its face, the road runs down past the parish church to the Ship Canal and the Mersey. Early in the nineteenth century Runcorn was a 'place of resort for salt-water bathing, the fine air and the pleasantness of the neighbourhood contributing useful auxiliaries to the effects of the bath'. Considerable numbers of invalids from Manchester and Liverpool 'resport to the place in the summer months for the sake of the sea bathing and the enjoyment of the air which is reckoned particularly salubrious'. The Runcorn of three hundred years ago consisted of nothing but 'a fair parish church, a vicarage and a few scattered tenements'. The Duke's canal played a big part in changing all that. The chemical industry arose, the Ship Canal arrived and Runcorn the health resort became Runcorn the seaport.

I turned my back on the bridge and the moon and headed under the Doctor's Bridge and off into the sun. The mist still played around the boats, the frost stuck to the grass, the sun peeped uncertainly over the houses as if it might be late. The view was compelling. I looked out over the cobbled lane running alongside the canal, over the river that had so little water it looked possible to walk across to Widnes where the chimneys and towers were puffing away cheerily. I knew the remains of Norton Priory were not too far away, towards the river, snug in woodland, once a prosperous monastery with an abbot who did not take at all kindly to King Henry VIII's covetous approach. The sheriff, Sir Piers Dutton, scattered the monks and their helpers and in his report to the King, in which he told of his capture of the abbot and three canons, he said the company had fled 'and some of them took to pooles and wateres and it was so dark I could not fynd them.' The King sent him 'right harty thanks' and ordered the hangings.

The path was closed at Preston Brook Marina, and I had to pick my way through the new housing estate on the other side of the canal, heading for the M56 motorway and hurrying shiftily past an old notice forbidding admittance to a lane except on business, and over the bridge where the canal splits, the left hand to Manchester, the right hand to the Trent and Mersey Canal. There were no disturbing notices from the other direction, the path was well trodden and I soon lost my feeling of guilt over ignoring the sign. I smiled contentedly to myself and looked into the sky, its deep blue broken only by a few cotton wool clouds and the trailing, dispersing slip stream of a jet aircraft. The cooling towers were still dominating the scene, three hours after I had first seen them, in the dark as I passed on the train.

As I walked under George Gleaves bridge, I made a mental note to discover who the man was. I never did. I had forgotten him as soon as I started across the fields, up a wooded hillside to drop into Daresbury, the village where Lewis Carroll, creator of *Alice in Wonderland*, was born. I strolled past the Cobbler's Cottage and wished I had taken Latin at school so I could have made sense of the inscription on the wall which faces the road up to the church where a Lewis Carroll window was installed as a memorial to him to commemorate the centenary of his birth in 1832. Charles Ludwidge Dodgson, the son of the rector of All Saints, was born in the parsonage at Newton-by-Daresbury two miles away. The building was destroyed by fire in 1883 but a photograph remains, taken by Lewis Carroll himself on a return visit to Daresbury about 1860. A copy of the original is inside the church. The original, for some reason, is in Princeton University, New Jersey, among a collection of his photographs.

Lewis Carrol did not marry but was fond of children and would no doubt be delighted to learn of the great number of girls who have been baptized Alice in Daresbury. The stained glass window in the church depicts several of the characters from his most famous work, the white rabbit and the dodo, the mock turtle and the mad hatter, the queen and the duchess, and the reminder of home, the Cheshire Cat. But I should have looked closer. I missed the man himself.

> I'd give all wealth that years have piled,
> The slow result of Life's decay,
> To be once more a little child
> For one bright summer-day.

Not quite a summer-day, but the sun was still sparkling on the canal as it moved through quiet country, past Moore and Higher Walton, past Walton Hall Garden with its picnic area, playground, pets' corner, pond, pitch and putt. And bandstand. A four-storey warehouse signals the approach of Stockton Quay and London Bridge from where the packet boats used to leave for Manchester. The old packet boat steps are still there, and an illustration outside the London Bridge pub shows the boat ready to leave as the Liverpool stage-coach arrives with more passengers. The service ran from 1771 until after 1918, and the pub, blacksmith's, Bank Riders House, warehouse and agent's house remain from those days.

The Ship Canal is not too far away, at Stockton Heath, where the Bridgewater joins up with the Manchester to Chester road, wandering along the edges of Warrington, past lovely old property until the two part company at Grappenhall. Houses still looked out on the water but everywhere was quiet and perfect – my sort of fishing day with an armchair at the water's edge, a Lewis Carroll book, a bottle of anything to keep out any unexpected chill, a bulging picnic basket and, if you really insisted, a rod. One particularly old man was fishing in the shade of a chestnut tree. His overcoat was threadbare and he hunched his shoulders as he rubbed his hands together to give them more warmth. He looked as if he had not shaved for a week but blue eyes sparkled out of the weather-beaten face as he concentrated on the water. A small stove and a pan waited nearby. This man was not fishing for fun or to pass the time of day. He was hunting for food and had no time for my over-cheery nonsense about the lovely day for the time of year.

A small aqueduct marked 'Thelwall Underbridge' reminded me I was nearing the mighty Thelwall viaduct where the M6 motorway is carried over the Ship Canal. Mind you, if you want a gentler way to cross the Ship Canal, there is still the Thelwall Ferry where passengers and dogs are transported for a ha'penny (including return on same day!). It is rather more expensive if you have a bicycle or pram as well. Then it becomes a penny. Once under the motorway, it is not far to the delightful town of Lymm with its winding, hilly streets, its stocks and cross and square. The canal runs through the centre, and there can be nowhere better to eat or drink than the Bull's Head, right on the bridge by Bridgewater House.

The Ship Canal takes itself off on a gentle curve as it looks to enter Manchester from the west. The Bridgewater, however, stays in Cheshire as long as it can, through quiet countryside, past old cottages freshly coated with white paint, lovely cottages

Cobbled alley at Lymm, leading to the Bridgewater Canal.

with small windows, tall chimneys, porches with wistaria wandering over them. Something rather larger appears on the right as Dunham Massey Hall comes into view over the meadows, standing in a wooded park with deer and an Elizabethan mill by the River Bollin. The canal skirts Altrincham, and although it tenaciously continues to cling to the country, I could make out the start of the Manchester sprawl over the flats directly ahead. By Broadheath, the industry has arrived. The Linotype Works 1897 looms large; a huge, derelict works overlooking the canal has lost every window – twelve hundred of them smashed. Once past Timperley railway station, the canal starts its long straight run to Sale, flanked by houses and the railway line heading for Manchester Piccadilly. Under the M63 and over the Mersey, a much more modest river here.

Once past Stretford Station, the canal swings left to Waters Meeting where the original main line of the canal is joined. Its most interesting part is the section through Worsley and past the site of the Duke's coal mines, the inspiration for the canal. The ten-mile branch ends at Leigh where it runs into the Leeds and Liverpool Canal.

After swinging right at Waters Meeting, the main line of the Bridgewater, now fast running out of towpath, swings round Manchester United's football ground of Old Trafford as it sneaks into the city. The path, which had been excellent throughout twenty-six or twenty-seven miles, was now either fenced off or non-existent, although it was possible to get onto the bank in one or two parts. On the other side of United's ground, where only a road separates the Bridgewater and the Ship Canal, is a magnificent mural on a gable end for Manchester Haulage and Warehousing, depicting industry, ships, cranes and, of course, a scene from Old Trafford. And that just has to be Denis Law scoring one of his many wonderful goals. It was around this spot, where the last three docks were positioned, that the old Pomona Gardens stood before the arrival of the Ship Canal. There was a zoo, a concert hall and a lovers' walk; people arrived by boat as well as by road, and when people like John Bright and Benjamin Disraeli were speaking, there were audiences of over twenty thousand. The canal is now close to Castlefield Junction, the end of the Bridgewater but the beginning of the Rochdale Canal with its link with the Ashton and Peak Forest Canals. Here once was a busy canal basin with wharves and warehouses and much activity. Now, just the occasional flash of life treads over the grave of a once thriving industry. I wonder what Lewis Carrol would have made of it.

> I see the shadows falling,
> The forms of old recalling;
> Around me tread the mighty dead,
> And slowly pass away.

DISTANCE OF WALK: 28 MILES.   **OS MAP 108 and 109**

20

Rochdale Canal

The ghosts are everywhere. They come out of the crypts of Castlefield in the depths of Manchester, roam the ruins of the ancient hall by the water, walk the walls of the mills. There are no barriers. Yorkshire, Lancashire, woollen, cotton, brick, stone, hills, vales, they wander, they wail. They will not go. The imprints of their clammy fingers show at every turn.

There is Clegg Hall, 350 years old, just out of Rochdale. For fifty years it has been dying, crumbling, withering, decaying. The old war-horse, forgotten and neglected but still on its feet, scorning the last act of death. Its empty windows gape out over the canal and railway, unseeing, hollow eyes deep in the skull. Caved floors, open but unwelcome doors, treacherous steps, ceiling upon ceiling that let in the sky, rotting beams, giant stones jumbled and cracked. But as always there is life in death. Toadstools in the sodden wood, mould on the stones, bushes and weeds spreading to cover the shame. The parapets point defiantly to God, and water trickles from the channelled stone spouts, so many tongues sticking out from the top of the building. Children determined to have the last word. The front door, once proud and inviting, is boarded and barbed, the porches stand at the back, one with the date 1637 showing signs of erosion. When it was erected, the Civil War was almost upon England.

A mill stands near the hall, a mill and four workers' houses, once eight until the dividing walls were knocked down. The stray visitor could easily feel unwelcome. Dogs with bared teeth and hungry eyes strained at leashes. Their barking would waken the dead. And there have been a few of those at Clegg Hall, one or two murdered, so the story goes.

Legend has it that, about six or seven hundred years ago, in the days of the original hall, built in the twelfth century, a wicked uncle, guardian of two orphaned heirs, threw them into the moat to deny them their inheritance and to claim it for himself. For

The boarded-up entrance to Clegg Hall, 350 years old,
on the banks of Rochdale Canal.

hundreds of years, even after the hall had been replaced by the
present building, the place was haunted by what was known as
the Clegg-Ho Boggart. Edwin Waugh, the famed Lancashire
writer of the last century, said the ghost remained the theme of
many stories among the people who lived near the hall. There
was even a proverb: 'Ah'm here again – like Clegg-Ho Boggart.'

Clegg Hall is about fourteen miles from Manchester, where the
Rochdale Canal links with the Bridgewater. They join at Castlefield, once a wharf, once part of the camp set up by the Romans at
Mancunium. This was an area throbbing with life when the canal
age was at its height. Today it is a spot for the historian, to sit and
imagine and gaze out at precious little, perhaps watch the occasional boatman venture through the Cheshire Ring which takes
in the Bridgewater Canal and the first mile and a quarter of the
Rochdale Canal. The Rochdale was a worker from the start. From
the moment it was born, a truly aristocratic birth through the
Duke's Lock, it was subject to the demands of the mills and
factories and warehouses which overpowered it and threatened
to squeeze the life out of it.

Deansgate, one of the city's busy thoroughfares, was bustling with life. Two hundred yards away, down Castle Street, it was quiet, almost creepy, a step back into Victorian times, even beyond. I went to Castlefield just as dawn was breaking. The canal was empty. Well, almost. Wrecks of old barges settle uneasily in the mud. One has almost completely disintegrated, but its rudder fights on gamely. The high walls help to deepen the eerie atmosphere, windows are broken and boarded, grass and weeds sprout from the drainpipes and gulleys. For a mile and a quarter the canal makes its way through the centre of commercial Manchester, under Deansgate, Oxford Street, Princess Street, London Road, alongside Whitworth Street, Canal Street, past the Refuge building and Piccadilly Station, through nine locks and a few tunnels. Much of the way is cobbled, and through one narrow old tunnel the feel of the cobbles under my feet reminded me of my youth, when every street in Lancashire seemed to have been made that way. Some of the buildings are still being used but others are derelict, even dangerous, their insides on show to the world. Even a huge, brick chimney stands at Bloom Street, and a reminder of the canal age comes at the mill with the loading bays and the mooring rings set in the wall. For a short stretch the towpath leaves the canal side and takes to the street – Canal Street of course. In a book on the Rochdale Canal there is a lovely picture of a heavily laden flat barge being pulled by a horse in Canal Street, its minder walking by its side, his arms behind his back, two boys in caps following. And the mills and warehouses all around. That street still has its cobbled footpath, but now it has parking meters, too.

After Canal Street the canal takes one more dive under the city before it is out in the open. I hopped over the wall at the other side of Minshull Street Bridge and was soon underground on the narrow cobbled path, beneath a low-arched bridge and into the tunnel, with its strip lighting, leading to Piccadilly and Dale Street Locks. I clung on to the cold iron railing, passed Piccadilly Lock and emerged into a basin where sunken columns stand in the water, supporting the building and car-park above. For a moment I dreamed I was in Athens. But no . . . a rusty little boat peeped out of a tunnel to remind me exactly where I was, under London Road, somewhere near Joshua Hoyle's ('Celebrated Fabrics') old warehouse, beautiful red and white terracotta, now empty and

Rochdale Canal in the centre of Manchester.

dirty, for sale or rent. It was 8.30 and people were hurtling down the slope from Piccadilly Station. Nearly time for work, nearly time for work, nearly time for work. I quickly escaped, back underground, under the office building of 111 Piccadilly, under its car-park and up the path and through the small stout door that looks to have been there for ever and which leads on to Dale Street. The lock at Dale Street is the ninth and last in the mile and a quarter. And for that people in boats paid £16. The navigable Cheshire Ring continues along the Ashton Canal branching off to the right, but the Rochdale forks left past the car-park alongside the Rochdale Canal Company building. I walked through the car-park and across a wooden bridge, the first of many low bridges that have been thrown across this waterway.

At least I was in the open. I celebrated by going on to a quaint iron bridge, humped and dating from 1838. A men's lavatory stands nearby, twelve feet high, white stoned like a marble palace, flushed only by the rain. The towpath returns to the canal side by way of a roving bridge and tunnel, and now the industry and high buildings start to thin out, the housing at Ancoats and Miles Platting threatening to take over. A pub, the Navigation, stands alongside one of the many locks that have been filled in and stepped, and its sign shows a rural scene, trees and fields, a horse and barge. Quite different from now.

For a time the path was blocked, forcing me to leave the canal and go down Coleshill Street with its blue pavement and road from the Manox chemical works. But I was soon able to return to the canal at the end of the street, back to the low concrete bridges and on to Newton Heath, where a recent housing development has honoured Manchester United footballers killed in the plane crash at Munich in 1958. It was market day at Newton Heath, a good old outdoor Lancashire market held on Mondays, Wednesdays and Saturdays, right next to the canal. It was too good to resist, and I did not leave until I had seen every stall and sampled a bacon barm cake and a quarter of chocolate fudge.

The canal wanders uncertainly into Failsworth, past huge mills and the Home Guard Club before vanishing under the Shopping Giant supermarket. 'Are they still guarding us from the last war or is this for the next?' I asked a man outside the Home Guard Club. 'Nay, it's for th' Old Comrades,' he answered seriously. The canal re-emerges a hundred yards up the main Oldham Road, just past the 'Carnegie Free Library', and at last I felt I was leaving industry behind. For once, the walls were not squeezing in, and the overpowering presence of the mills – the canal used to serve five in a quarter of a mile near the supermarket – was being left behind. Not that it can be called beautiful. The railway line is near, a gasometer, a works and a tip are at hand, and Chadderton power station looms. Still, it is open and the Pennines, over which the canal has to go in ten miles time, are coming ever closer. More enormous mills appear at Chadderton, and the pylons, apparently chained to the canal, provide company past Middleton Junction, Chadderton Fold, Boarshaw (no relation), and up to the top Laneside Lock at Slattocks. But just when you think the country is truly opening out, when the pylons are taking off for Bacup and Darwen and anywhere, just when there are a few fields around, the M62 motorway comes into sight.

A lane under the motorway links the two cut ends of the canal, which is broken again by another motorway tentacle at the bottom of Rochdale, a small market town in medieval times, a woollen town at one time, a busy cotton town in recent times. The co-operative movement started here, and John Bright, who fought for industrial reform, was born here. The canal sees only the edges of Rochdale, through council flats, past Well i' th' Lane, touching Comet and Kwik Save, and crossing the main road to Oldham between two pubs with names deeply attached to the area, the Red Rose and Bishop Blaize, the patron saint of wool-combers. Birch Hill Hospital appears in sight in the valley with its distinctive clock tower before the sad face of Clegg Hall heralds the noise of the large Armour Hess chemical works on the edge of the small town of Littleborough. Now for the Pennines.

Twelve locks lift the canal from Littleborough to the Summit, climbing into the Pennines and quickly into Yorkshire. The hills close in as the canal searches for the gaps. Sheep cling to the steep sides; dry stone walls claw their way to the hilltops. It is quiet and bleak and cold. And lonely. Longlees Lock No. 36 starts the canal on its way down again, and on the hill to the left is a ventilation shaft for the railway which drives its way through the hill with the Summit Tunnel. The canal drops towards the spire of Walsden parish church. One old lock gate sprouts grass, water gushes through the holes, rhododendrons have rooted near the top of another lock chamber. Geese and heather line the banks.

I once read the Rochdale Canal described as beautiful. This is only half true. The half that is in Yorkshire. And I cannot help thinking that all the canals in Lancashire have their most beautiful parts in other counties, the Leeds and Liverpool in Yorkshire, the Bridgewater in Cheshire. The lock in the centre of Todmorden, a small town once half in Yorkshire and half in Lancashire but now wholly in Yorkshire, has been carefully and thoughtfully

Signposts on the Rochdale Canal, between
Littleborough and Todmorden.

restored, part of a scheme 'inaugurated by the Mayor of Calderdale, 8 September 1982'. The area has been cobbled; there are benches and a garden which include an original milestone from the canal: 'S 10. Manr 22.' So. Ten miles to Sowerby Bridge. Two Indian restaurants, the Taj Mahal and the Bombay, flank the bridge over the canal, but the path is through a delightful, narrow, low stone tunnel under the road.

The valley floor opens out. The hills move over, and the River Calder, which soon forms its own Navigation with the River Hebble, is working itself up into a decent size as it accompanies the canal towards Sowerby Bridge. Some of the towline grooves in the bridges are quite deep, and some of the wooden rollers, installed to protect the stone and rope, are still in position. One of them, which looks as if it has not rolled too well, is almost eaten through by the towrope. The land is pretty and wooded around Shaw Bridge, and soon the hills close in again, leaving just enough room for the river, canal, road and railway. They all roll on together through the attractive little town of Hebden Bridge with its antique shops and its four- and five-storey houses set against the hills and past the now unusual sight of a factory making and selling clogs. It seemed as if everybody wore clogs when I was a boy in Lancashire, and how we made the sparks fly as we kicked the irons on the pavement. The snow would pack on the soles, too, and I often grew two inches in the few hundred yards to school.

The canal leaves behind Mytholmroyd, Luddenden Foot and the lovely-sounding Friendly as it nears its end. Terraced cottages back on to the canal and river with railed balconies. The washing blew and waved over the rails, eager to break free and fly along the valley, through the tunnel cut in the rock, past Puzzle Hall Inn and into Sowerby Bridge, where the canal ends at the car-park for Kwik Save. The man from Sunblest was just arriving.

The canal used to go on past Christ Church in the centre of the town and into the basin where it linked with the Calder and Hebble Navigation. As I wandered along past the moored boats, a man stopped to tell me how his grandfather used to empty coal from the barges there for 't' gas 'ouse'. 'They had a horse here, a grey, eighteen hands, from t' brewery, and before they altered this bridge there were an iron pipe standing on t' path. Horse would go round it, come back up t' path on its own and into t' stable while t' boat floated on to its mooring. It's still Rochdale Canal here though there's some calls it Calder and Hebble. That's what it is further on. But how can you say where one starts and another ends? It's all watter. If you can call it watter,' he added, staring at the dark waters of the canal.

DISTANCE OF WALK: 33 MILES.   **OS MAPS 103, 104 and 109**

21

Leeds and Liverpool Canal

The complete contrast between the ends of the Leeds and Liverpool Canal came home to me as I entered the final mile of the 127-mile waterway in Liverpool. I had been on my own for miles, hemmed in by factory walls, fastened in by locked bridge gates, when I came across a dog in the canal, barking loudly, his paws up on the stone slabs at the edge of the towing path. He was an ugly beggar, almost a bull terrier, with a strong, sturdy body, little pricked ears and tiny, appealing eyes. His paws were raw and bleeding from trying to escape, and two men, working at the nearby Stanley Dock where the canal links with the River Mersey, decided he had been thrown in. 'They do that sort of thing round here, you know,' said one. The surroundings, the atmosphere, were so different from the Leeds end, which has its industry, of course, but which does not squeeze in on the canal like a vice. The countryside opens out within three miles for a long, delightful stretch of water. And I was still on the edges of Leeds when I saw a kingfisher.

River Lock, where the canal joins the Aire and Calder Navigation, is so close to Leeds City Station that the announcements come through loud and reasonably clear. There are some fine old warehouses, and an arm of the canal actually disappears under the station – 'And the next boat to arrive at platform five will be the 7.30 to Liverpool, arriving on Thursday . . .' Two hundred yards further along is Office Lock and the grand canal office building with its clean stone blocks and the Car Acts notice of 1896 and 1903 refusing to allow more than five tons to go past.

The start to the canal is clear and impressive, so different from its Liverpool end, with a spotless towpath that looks as if it has just been hoovered. The first bridge is numbered 226! A long way to go. The River Aire, which accompanies the canal for over thirty miles, is close at hand, and a slice of land only twenty yards wide separates the two waters at the start. There are six locks in the first mile, two of them forming the first of eight sets of staircase locks

A warehouse at Liverpool, near the end of
the Leeds and Liverpool Canal.

in the first seventeen miles, climaxing in the spectacular five-rise at Bingley. Unlike the usual locks with pounds in between, the chambers of the staircase locks open into each other so that the top gate of the bottom lock is the bottom gate of the next lock and so on, thus saving on building costs and water. Not to mention the effort of getting through them. The sixth lock in the opening mile lifts the canal well above the Aire, extending the vista for miles with a skyline of spires and mill chimneys. In one ninety-degree arc I counted eight church spires in such places as Burley, Woodhouse, Meanwood, Headingley and Horsforth. The variety of chimneys more than matches the spires, some square, some squat, red brick, blackened brick, one with a narrowed, pencil top, another cement white with a black tip. A giant cigarette.

After the river has taken off round the other side of a generating station, the canal grows another arm, about three hundred yards long with lots of strong iron mooring posts and two great old barges rotting away deep in the water. The industry on the right contrasts with the lovely woodland of Armley, Gotts and Wither Parks on the left, countrified enough for a kingfisher which flitted along in front of me for ten minutes before turning back. I managed to get within twenty-five yards as it sat on a branch and watched me from across the water, its chestnut front mixing easily with the autumn leaves, its sharp, shrill call at odds with the clear, loud song of the wrens on the towpath. What a lovely send-off.

A sign for a pickles factory at Amen Corner leads on to Kirkstall Bridge, one I cross many times on the way to Kirkstall Lane and Headingley, the home of Yorkshire cricket just over a mile away. Much more impressive though, as ever, is the sight across the fields and over the river, of Kirkstall Abbey, so much of it so well preserved. There, in the middle of trim lawns and near to the river, stands the church, which has lost only parts of the roof and the tower in its eight hundred years. It is well worth seeing, an extensive abbey that had the usual monastic buildings such as dormitories and cloisters, warming house, kitchen, refectory, chapter house. I looked down from the canal, thrilled yet again at the gritstone church with its bold tower. A market gardener was at work close by, gulls were screeching round, and I looked beyond the abbey to the main road to Ilkley and Skipton, to the houses climbing up Kirkstall Lane.

The Bingley five-rise staircase locks.

It came as a surprise to find the canal empty of water at the other side of Kirkstall Lock. 'It's a beggar, isn't it?' puffed a short, wizened man with a greyhound. 'There'll be no barges in here now. And there's been nowt in t' paper.' But this was the close season on the canal, with lots of repair work going ahead on locks, bridges, banks and the canal bed itself. The surroundings become pleasant although the canal is to stay close to towns for many miles yet. A grey squirrel hurried for the safety of a tree in Bramley Fall Woods, set in the crook of the arm created by the river and canal making a sharp turn to the left. The Abbey Inn sits on the bridge over the Aire downhill from the canal just after the staircase locks of Forge and Newlay which marked the end of the dry stretch. I peeped over the wall at the remains of a huge mill before reaching another blockage, created by a metal swing bridge being erected to replace a heavy wooden one at Ross Mill. A temporary footbridge had been slung across a barge. I could not resist. I walked across and back, much to the interest of the workmen.

It is not far to the little canal town of Rodley with its nearby pubs, the Rodley Barge and the Owl, and there is a welcoming warmth about the entire place. I find this almost everywhere in Yorkshire. I can only think it must be the stone buildings, weathered, warm, with a strong suggestion of permanency. The country is lovely here, trees and fields everywhere, with a gully on the left opening up a view of the church tower at Calverley and a succession of woods emphasizing the quiet.

The railway line, which also keeps reasonably close company from Leeds, crosses both the river and the canal before burrowing its way into a hill. Both waters, however, have to find their way round, leaving the small town of Idle on the left as they go. I have a particular affection for this small town for I used to visit here to see Eddie Paynter, the man who played cricket for Lancashire and England in the 1930s and who became a hero when he left his sickbed in Brisbane to help England win a Test match. I never could understand what a busy little Lancastrian was doing in a Yorkshire town called Idle.

A delightful stretch opens out to Shipley, with the Aire often cuddling up close, the Baildon Moor providing a lovely backcloth for a canal which goes through another three-lock staircase at Field Locks. It was here, just before Shipley, that I saw my first milestone. I had seen plenty of posts bearing simply '½' but here was the first real, genuine mile post, iron, triangular shaped, with Liverpool 115 miles, Leeds 12¼ miles. Bridge 208 soon follows, the connection with the ill-fated Bradford Arm of the canal, completed in 1774 and which ran nearly four miles to the city. It was a great boon to Bradford in its early days, but after becoming 'a seething cauldron of all impurity', being drained for five years then restored, it was finally abandoned in 1922. There is not much of it to be seen now apart from the start of the arm just outside Shipley, with its wharves, warehouses, boats and offices, a reminder of the enormous part the canal played in the development of the town.

Within a few minutes I was approaching Saltaire, a combination of the name of the man who established the place, Sir Titus Salt, and the river Aire. Like Mr Cadbury, who dreamed up the village of Bournville, near Birmingham, Sir Titus believed in good working conditions for his workers. So as well as building his mill, he put up houses, schools, library, baths, a Congregational church and almshouses. Clean air, decent living conditions . . . but no pub. The mill is on both sides, six storeys high, vast, a piece of industrial grandeur. Broken windows on one side, blocked windows on the other, and pulleys high in the sky to pull the goods up six floors. I wandered through the streets, some of which had been named after Sir Titus's children. There is George and Edward, Albert and Herbert and Fanny, but if all the streets reflect the number of his children, he must have been a prolific producer. The houses look strong and stylish, several of them, especially at the ends, carrying an extra storey. A man was photographing the beautiful and distinctive old Congregational church, now the Saltaire United Reformed church with its impressive pillared, rounded entrance.

I crossed the bridge over the canal and the neighbouring river into the park with its boathouse and café, where stew and dumplings were on the menu. There is a statue in the park to Sir Titus, baronet, founder of Saltaire, heavily bearded, in a frock coat and with what I thought was a scroll in his hand. I later read this was a piece of cloth, while on the plinth below are engraved the angora and alpaca goats from which the Salt Mills materials were made. The statue, by F. Derwent Wood of London, was erected in 1903 to commemorate the hundredth anniversary of Sir

Titus's birth and the fiftieth anniversary of the opening of the mills.

I was soon back on the canal bank, in a woody, shaded region leading to the aqueduct over the Aire, itself as still as a canal here. 'I hear they're working on t' five rise,' a man offered as we passed in the shadow of a warehouse, on the side of which I could just make out the words 'Leeds and Liverpool Canal Company'. But the three-rise staircase locks come first. A path runs away to the nearby church where the clock was just striking one, and across the fields I could see the five-rise, an impressive feature of the canal. Work was going on. A crane sat awkwardly on the hill, helmeted workmen buzzed around busily, all watched by a succession of passers-by. From the top I looked down on mills and chimneys and across to the hills. A plaque is set in rock. 'This plaque commemorates the bi-centenary of the Bingley Five-Rise Locks. 21 March 1974.' I was high enough to look down into people's bedrooms but that was nothing compared with the lovely moorland, the fields and woods, the stone buildings, ages-old farms. Even industry cannot intrude. The valley is too wide and open to let it take over.

It was time for refreshment and I chose the Marquis of Granby overlooking the water at Stockbridge just as the landlord and a customer were deep in reminiscences about their footballing days. The tears were rolling down their cheeks. 'Remember that night when George had a few too many. It were a wonder we got him on t' field following day. First tackle and he fell flat on his back and we had to carry him off.' . . . 'And what about Mrs Brown who used to take her umbrella to t' matches and then lay about t' referee with it.' . . . 'We used to have to carry t' goal posts up to t' top field for every game. By time we got them up, it was time for us tea.'

Soon after leaving the Marquis, I was alongside Keighley golf course with two holes climbing out of the valley for a place right next to the canal. Industry falls behind for a while to leave a patch of pure Airedale country with its rhododendrons and dry stone walls, broken briefly by the small town of Silsden and a 1911 notice still warning that, 'Proceedings will be taken against persons cycling or otherwise trespassing on the towing path.' The ancient church of St Andrew's – 'The Lang Kirk o' Craven. AD 950' – stands close to the canal at Kildwick where the Aire comes in close before taking off for the delightful Yorkshire market town of Skipton.

It was still dark when I returned to Skipton the following morning. It was market day, half past six, and many of the stall-holders had already arrived. The heavy thump of barrows over cobbles, the clang of metal poles, the calls of traders brought a noisy end to the quiet of the night. The broad High Street was wide awake, watched over by the magnificent castle and the church, squat towered and square bodied. The past is ever present in the centre of Skipton. The Black Horse still has its mounting block, and plaques recall the days of bull-baiting, the toll booth and prison cells 'where felons were incarcerated and branded', the pillory, taken down in 1770, the market cross and stocks which were removed in 1840. The activity was too much for two mallards, who decided to return to the canal after a wander round town. A motorist slowed as they crossed the Leeds road. I accompanied them down to the water and set my face in the direction of Lancashire, fifteen miles away.

It does not take long to find the country with fine views of Carleton and Elslack moors on one side and Sharp How and its woodland on the other. A milepost told me I was now less than a hundred miles from Liverpool although between Skipton and Gargrave I was heading in the wrong direction. But that is one of the delights of a canal. It has places to go, so while the journey by motorway between Leeds and Liverpool is only about seventy-five miles, by canal it is 127. Some of those extra miles are well worthwhile on the way to Gargrave, a charming spot with low stone cottages with undulating roofs. The Old Swan has a pillared entrance, the brown-stone church is from the sixteenth century, and houses are linked through the ages. The war memorial records that thirty-eight men of the village died in the First World War, eight in the Second. There are some lovely names: Danson Yeoman, Riley Chew, Ben Dobby.

The canal, which goes under the road to the Lakes when it leaves the village, soon says farewell to the Aire at the Priest Holme Aqueduct, after thirty-five miles together. Six locks at Gargrave, six more at Banknewton, the canal twisting like a grass snake, mile upon mile of quiet walking, and I felt I was on the roof of Yorkshire with picturesque panoramas over windswept moorlands and green fields. Between Banknewton and Greenberfield

The double-arched bridge at East Marton on
the Leeds and Liverpool Canal.

Locks is a peaceful five-mile length known as Marton Pool,
broken by one major road which crosses the canal on a curious
double-arched bridge, one arch on top of the other when the level
of the road was raised. Here is the village of East Marton with its
Cross Keys Inn and St Peter's Church, where the Hebers of
Marton Hall and the Roundells of nearby Gledstone have clearly
played a large part in its history. A monument to Reginald Heber,

who died in 1715, declares: 'Married Esther, daughter of Sir William Cayley of Brompton Bar and left her a widow with 10 children, four of which died under age, the rest all married except Rebecca Heber who desired this monument might be put up in remembrance of so good and pious parents.'

The canal reaches its summit more than two miles on, with the three Greenberfield Locks which lift it to nearly five hundred feet above sea level. These locks were put there in 1820 to replace the original flight, and the old dry bed can be seen to the right, leaving the strange sight, three hundred yards away, of a bridge straddled over nothing, but turned into what looks like a stable incorporated in the bridge arch. A straight run into Barnoldswick aims for Weets Hill, standing over a town with blocks of dull grey houses, works, chimneys, foundry, two Rolls-Royce plants and the bed-manufacturing concern Silentnight. In a little over a mile I was at the border, stepping from Yorkshire into Lancashire, past the canal feeder that marks the dividing line. I was safe! Back among Lancashire houses, Lancashire hills and Lancashire dogs barking their heads off. Just over forty-four miles of the canal are in Yorkshire, the remaining eighty-three in Lancashire.

Foulridge Tunnel, nearly a mile long, was only twenty minutes away, a tunnel famous in canal circles for the feat of a cow which fell in the water at the Barrowford end and swam to the Foulridge end, where it was rescued and revived with brandy. I had read that a photograph of the cow was displayed in the Hole in the Wall Inn. That I had to see, so I walked up Warehouse Lane, just before the tunnel, and into the pub. I was directed into the back room, the General Room, where the photograph, framed, hangs on the wall. The unnamed cow, pictured in sepia, dutifully looks at the camera. 'This cow, owned by Mr R. Brown, Blue Slate Farm, swam the full length of Foulridge Mile Tunnel September 24th 1912.' The paper surround to the picture is browning, and it is hard to tell what breed of cow performed this great feat. 'I've never altered it in twenty-five years,' said the landlord. 'Never had it blown up, coloured or painted. That's the original and I think it would spoil it.'

I left the pub and followed the road towards Barnoldswick, going along Reedymoor Lane, the way the horses went. I went through a Waterways Board gate, imagining the horses clopping through the lanes while the barge men legged the vessel through the tunnel. An elderly man with a red setter and a peke was near the Barrowford end of the tunnel. He recalled horses being put in a small nearby field, resting, waiting to resume duty. 'It must be twenty-five years ago, maybe more,' he thought. 'They'd stay with the same boat all the way up. They couldn't take the horses across the railway level crossing here; they had to take them down this lane and under the line. Funny, isn't it? Here was the railway and the canal together, both busy, main lines of transport. Now both have gone. Never to return.' He said the tunnel was 'straight as a die' and he was right. I leaned over the entrance and could see the pin-point of light at the other end.

Early in the afternoon I got my first glimpse from the towpath of Pendle Hill, its solid mass dominating this north-eastern part of the county. Pendle is something special for me, having lived in its shadow for several years and being brought up on a diet of witches and spells, of Mother Demdike and Alice Nutter. Pendle stays in sight for a few miles as the canal starts its journey downhill, through Barrowford Locks, across Colne Water and jostling with Pendle Water for several miles as it runs along the back of Nelson towards Burnley. The open country has gone. Industry closes in on dismal surroundings. This is where I was born, so this is special for me, even its long factory walls with a hundred downspouts, its hills of coal and sand and mortar, even Brierfield Gasworks Tip and the cooling towers of Padiham Power Station. For looming over everywhere is dear old Pendle, squatting behind the Forest of Pendle like the hump of a whale.

Dusk had arrived by the time I reached Burnley. I walked on over the River Brun which gave the town its name, through Queen's Park and Thompson's Park, on to the mighty embankment, three-quarters of a mile long, which carries the canal over the valley that holds the centre of the town. The floodlights of Burnley's Turf Moor football ground were behind me, but in front lay the town. There was the supermarket, all brightly lit up, the Keirby Hotel standing high in the centre, the recreation centre and there . . . the bus station. The white and red lights of the vehicles twinkled and mixed with the yellow street lights of the roads to Manchester and Nelson and Blackburn. I could make out in the dusk light a church spire on the hill. The mill chimneys were hard to see. But then, there are not so many these days. Not as many as when I was a lad in this town.

The lights were still twinkling when I climbed up the embankment from the bus station the following morning. Burnley was coming to life, an hour or two later than in the days when weaving mills were prospering and the Wharf was a hive of industry. The Wharf was a toll point, and the toll house, with its railinged steps, still stands along with the canopied warehouses which stored such products as grain and sugar. Close by is a town landmark, Clock Tower Mill, crowned with Burnley's first public clock, put there in 1863. George Slater, who built the mill, also gave his name to a terrace, a row of houses with terracing above and alongside the warehouses. There were eleven houses, and the way in was along a walkway from the road bridge. It must have been a terrible place to live, yet now people want to preserve it as a museum. Burnley has changed enormously in the last thirty years. As I went past Barracks Station, I looked up at the old main road to Blackburn, now little more than a cul-de-sac side street to the vast new road system. The 599-yard Gannow tunnel, opened in 1801 after five years work, has lost much of its horse-path over the top, and after walking across Tunnel Street and up Boathorse Lane I found myself enmeshed in the tangle of roads. I went through the pedestrian way and passed St John the Baptist parish church down Gannow Lane and back to the canal near Bridge Inn.

It takes an hour to get into the country from the centre of Burnley. Not that anybody would call it pretty with its pylons and power stations and tips, but at least it is in the open. The cooling towers at Padiham stand to the right, those at Huncoat to the left, and the friendly bulk of Pendle Hill is still around. Those well-known contractors McAlpine and Fairclough, who were driving the M65 motorway through East Lancashire, apologized for any inconvenience caused to the waterway users. The sound of a clock striking the hour of nine drifted up through the valley from Padiham nearly two miles away, and I looked down into the town, afloat in the mist, its cooling towers puffing away, the smoke holding in the still air like balls of cotton wool.

A turn in the canal puts Padiham permanently to the rear, and two swing bridges, the first for nearly thirty miles, open the way to Clayton-le-Moors. An infants' school stands near the path, and for a while I watched little children rubbing their eyes and scratching their heads as they tried to cope with the mysteries of the alphabet. The canal, meanwhile, was having to cope with the mysterious spread of the M65. One of its feed roads, presumably from Accrington, caused a short diversion for the towpath before it returned to its own place with a bridge over the small branch, the Peel Arm. 'I don't know wheer I am,' said a fit-looking old man, striding out purposefully and swinging a walking-stick. 'They're carving t' countryside to pieces.'

The water itself was being diverted near Rishton in a fine stone channel. Not much chance of a leak there.

I had to wait a few minutes at Whitebirk on the edge of Blackburn while a concrete girder was lowered into position as part of a new motorway bridge. One of the helmeted young men pointed out that it was sometimes cheaper to divert a canal than build bridges over it. 'This canal twists so much it is often easier to straighten it out,' he said. The skyline around Whitebirk had changed a good deal from the last time I was there, for the generating station and its great cooling towers had been de-molished. The canal once passed within a few feet of the towers. Now there is nothing but open land. But not only had the power station gone: so had dear old Pendle after more than fifteen miles.

The canal ambles three miles through Blackburn, past the Thwaites and Whitbread breweries, both smack in the middle of town, behind the railway station, in front of the Infirmary with its six locks, over Ewood aqueduct with road and river beneath, and past Blackburn Rovers' Ewood Park ground with Darwen Tower high on the hill three miles away. And past a coal merchant's with the sign 'Dogs Keep Out'. Funny. I lived in Blackburn ten years but never realized how well-educated the animals were. I should have tried talking to one or two, I guess. As I approached Cherry Tree on the Preston side of Blackburn, I looked across to the Yellow Hills and the country park at Witton and the elegant tower of St Phillip's where I went as a boy.

Pleasant green land had returned, and I could make out the old castle on the hill at Hoghton as the canal entered its loveliest part since leaving Yorkshire. Through Mowden Woods, over Roddlesworth Aqueduct, along the Ollerton Valley to the flight of seven locks at Johnson's Hillock. On the left bank, about four miles from Chorley and sandwiched between the canal and the main road to Blackburn, is the village of Withnell Fold. The only approach, apart from by way of the canal, is down a pitted,

A factory at the water's edge in Blackburn.

pocked road which turns to cobbles just after the Methodist chapel. Stocks face the cottages and school which make up three parts of the square, and at the bottom of the village, approaching the mill, is a delightful little park.

Once through the locks the canal sets off on an eleven-mile run to Wigan, a stretch that was built as the southern end of the Lancaster Canal. The link-up through Preston was never achieved by the Lancaster Canal so this length was used by the Leeds and Liverpool who paid rent for the privilege until nationalization in 1948. The canal keeps company with the M61 motorway round the back of Chorley before moving through the pleasant Ridding Woods and past the cruise hire firm with such boat names of the area as *Rufford*, *Belmont*, *Angelzarke*, *White Coppice* and *Duxbury*. Another of the names, *Arley*, comes at the club house of Wigan Golf Club, once Arley Hall, a stately old mansion with a moat. *Haigh*, too, might have been among the names, for half an hour later comes Haigh Hall on the hill, with its tall, narrow windows looking down on the lawns and gardens, and the golfers, ideally positioned for losing the occasional ball.

Several anglers were on the bank with huge rods, black rods that looked more like telegraph poles, and two young hunters roamed about, popping away at anything that moved but thankfully missing. Wigan spread out to the right, and a man clutching bunches of flowers helped me out with the landmarks. 'Let's see. That church spire is St Pat's at Scholes, that's Westwood power station, the tower you can see is the parish church, and the floodlights belong to the Rugby League club. Good view isn't it? If it weren't so misty.'

The start of the impressive flight of twenty-three locks into Wigan marks the end of the old Lancaster Canal section, Aspull top lock opening the run downhill past the freshly painted Kirkless Hall Inn and the Commercial. The locks tumble down to Wigan, each identified with Roman numerals inside the chamber. They run under a busy main road close to St Pat's spire and pass a row of seven houses that make up Canal Terrace. They spread over 2½ miles, past the Leigh branch which links with the Bridgewater Canal seven miles away, and the power station I had first seen ninety minutes earlier. Iron clamps in the far wall at the junction with the Leigh branch mark where the rollers were positioned to protect the wall and the towrope itself.

The mere mention of 'Wigan Pier' was enough to get a laugh for the music-hall comedians. The thought that a town like Wigan in the heart of industrial Lancashire could have a pier tickled most people's fancy. Today there is no shortage of links with the pier, including a night club and even a Wigan Pier Heritage Centre. Another 'Wigan Pier Project' is at Trencherfield Mill near the bottom of the locks, a scheme by the council to provide an exhibition and design centre and renovate the mill engine. Yet Wigan Pier was nothing but a hump in the towpath opposite the Wharf. There horse-drawn passenger barges ran the thirty-five miles to Liverpool, an eight-hour journey that started at seven in the morning and which included a call at Scarisbrick, where passengers joined the stage-coach for the nearby seaside resort of Southport. But that was over a hundred years ago.

As the canal moves out of Wigan, the River Douglas, after an earlier brush with it, joins up again, a murky grey alongside the canal's muddy brown in an area of poor, unwanted wasteland. The two stay together for seven miles through Crooke and Gathurst and beneath the M6 motorway which towers over them. I arrived at Appley Bridge just in time to buy a programme at 'The Railway' for that afternoon's football match. I had not time to watch the game but moved on to Parbold with its beacon and its sailless windmill by the water. It was here, through an old farm, that I saw a cross, encircled by railings. 'Here stood old Douglas Chapel for four full centuries loved and thronged by those who worshipped God from all the country round. Existed 1526. Rebuilt 1621. Demolished 1875. The Holy Table, font and pulpit are now in Douglas Parish Church. This cross carved from the old threshold stone was erected July 1906. "Your fathers, where are they?"'

The lock at Appley Bridge is the last on the canal before Liverpool thirty miles away, and the land flattens out once the hills at Parbold have been left behind. The seven-mile-long Rufford Branch, where the canal locks into the River Douglas to flow into the Ribble Estuary, is just before Burscough Bridge. The branch flows through flat marshland and past Rufford Old Hall, a timber-framed manor house erected by the Hesketh family five hundred years ago. The basin at the start of the branch is an attractive spot with stout cottages gathered round a dry dock.

My fifth and final day on the Leeds and Liverpool started at Burscough Bridge the following morning. There was a great whiteness across the fields from the hard overnight frost, and the large, round moon which I had seen over the Pennines the previous night now lurked over the Irish Sea, unsmiling, staring frozenly. A jet plane's exhaust reflected the orange of the eastern sky, and geese, which might have had a restless night, oinked loudly as they flapped over Martin Mere Wildfowl Centre. It took the sun some time to get its head from under the covers, but once it had, the moon shrank under its glare and faded away.

The canal makes a semi-circle around the old town of Ormskirk from about two miles distant, the market centre of this rich agricultural district and an important coaching stage in the eighteenth century. And it skirts Scarisbrick Wood as it turns south for Lydiate and Maghull and the outskirts of Liverpool. There were lots of rustlings in the leaves, and a squirrel emerged, looking for breakfast. A heron, lifting from a stream in the wood, flew out twenty yards in front, somehow managing to miss hitting the trees and veering away like an aircraft banking to pick up the right direction. The geese, still moaning about the cold, flew overhead in the formation of a ragged tick. Perhaps geese, like some people, are not at their best first thing in the morning.

The canal is only a few miles from the coast, and I could see the Ainsdale and Birkdale Hills to the south of Southport. Through the trees I made out the spire of the church at Halsall, the village near where the first sod was cut on the canal, between bridges 23 and 24 near the 109-mile post. Charlie Mordaunt was the sod-cutter in November 1770, part of the section from Liverpool to Newburgh which opened five years later. The other end opened in 1777, with thirty-three miles from Leeds to Holmbridge near Gargrave, but it was 1816 before the sixty-six miles between were completely finished and the canal was opened for trade between Leeds and Liverpool. I am a great one for plaques, and I cannot help thinking that one to commemorate Mr Mordaunt and the start of a great canal would be worthwhile.

The towpath was closed at Downholland Bridge near the Scarisbrick Arms, but I was not too bothered. I had intended leaving the canal anyway to see the nearby ruins of St Catherine's Abbey in the fields at Lydiate. I climbed over a gate to see what was left of the church, fifty yards from the road. There is no roof, just the tower and walls, one with four windows, still standing. Brambles climb and cling, blocks of stone lie around, and one gravestone bears the words: 'Pray for the soul of Robert Lythgoe who departed this life November 21, 1861, aged 79 years.' Next door, and right handily placed, is the Scotch Pipers Inn, 1320, reputedly the oldest inn in Lancashire.

I returned to the canal just down the road and soon began to realize that the best was well behind me. There is not much in store from Maghull, where I first noticed the Scouse accents, though thirteen miles to Liverpool. A cluster of houses and a church, gathering together as if for warmth, make up Melling, and as the canal performs a huge U-turn, I could see Aintree and the neighbouring Old Roan long before I got there. My first glimpse of the Grand National racecourse at Aintree was through breaks in the fence close to one of the formidable jumps. Of course. This part would be Canal Turn. Then I came to the bridge that carries the road to the village of Melling. How many times had I heard: 'And now they are crossing the Melling road'? And sure enough, they do. Gates open on each side of the road, great wide gates to allow the Grand National horses through. Another familiar name comes as the canal passes Vernon's Pools, and now the bridges, and the number of miles to Liverpool, are down to single figures.

It was soon after Vernon's that I came to my first locked gate. 'There's been so many youngsters drowned,' a man explained to me. 'And then, there's the vandalism.' I found a way back onto the towpath through a break in the fence after two more locked gates and a wander through a housing estate. I soon wondered whether it was worth the effort. Rubbish and weeds were collecting, strong, high iron fencing lined the path, reinforced at a school with a close-knit second layer. There is open space near Crosby, but once into Litherland the canal is well and truly closed in for the remaining four miles.

It is a depressing end to a fine canal with pylons straddling the water – 'Danger. 132,000 volt lines. Central Electricity Generating Board.' The railings are twelve feet high, and I began to wonder if I would get out as the buildings closed right in on me. The sight of a church spire at Bootle seems incongruous, but there are more surprises to come with the sight of benches at the waterside. One faces a pylon and a wall of wasteland; the other looks on a derelict seven-storey building. Whoever would sit there? I thought. High walls and fencing, locked bridge gates – and benches? I could only think they had been misplaced. They should have been at the bus station. Then I heard the dog barking, my bull terrier in the water, and wished I was back in Yorkshire or Withnell Fold. Or even Burnley.

DISTANCE OF WALK: 127 MILES.   OS MAPS 102, 103 104 and 108

22

Lancaster Canal

The Lancaster is one of those canals that has been left completely cut off from the rest of the waterway system. It does have an outlet to the sea through Glasson Dock and the Lune Estuary, and judging by the size of many of the boats, it looks to be well used. But as an inland waterway, it is on its own, forty-two miles of it from Preston through Garstang and Lancaster to just beyond Carnforth. And it has been that way virtually all its life since being created in 1799. It was intended that the Lancaster should extend beyond Preston and on to Wigan, which would have given it a connection with the Leeds and Liverpool Canal. But the company never overcame the one big stumbling block, an aqueduct over the River Ribble at Preston. A horse tramway, which crossed the river on a wooden trestle bridge, linked the five-mile gap between the northern and southern sections while funds were gathered for the aqueduct. But they never came. The main-line railways finished off any lingering hopes, to leave part of the southern section continuing to be used by the Leeds and Liverpool, and part being abandoned. And the northern section, which then ran from Preston to Kendal, stayed on its own. Today it is navigable only to the locks at Tewitfield, four miles past Carnforth, but once out of Preston this is a lovely canal with unrivalled, spectacular views over Morecambe Bay and some quite special walking in Cumbria, up towards Kendal, out of reach of the boats.

The canal has been levelled for over half a mile in the centre of Preston, and the waterway now starts behind Shelley Road near bridge number 11, overlooked from a distance by the delicate, slender spire of St Walburga's and the tower of St Mark's. The bridge that soon takes the Blackpool traffic over the water is a remarkable feat of ugliness, so different from the delightful country stone bridges which are so much a feature of the canal.

Happily, the town is quickly left behind, the canal fringing Haslam Park as it heads for the Fylde and the quiet, unspoilt countryside, interrupted only by the crossing motorway to Blackpool. It passes over a succession of brooks that feed the Ribble or the Wyre, being carried over Barton Brook by a rather fine aqueduct with three lovely rounded arches, one of which has an unusual three-plank footpath running through the thirty-yard tunnel. The canal joins the A6 road to the north for a while, through Bilsborrow and Brock, under the road to the village of St Michael's on Wyre and over the Brock, a river with a delightful footpath, much of it through woodland, on the way towards the Bleasdale Fells. The Fells and the Forest of Bowland line the eastern side of the route north; the western side is flat right to the coast. It is nearly all grazing land, rural with little industry, just farms and cottages scattered around. The railway and the roads occasionally come close, but they are minor irritations. They all get together near the Green Man bridge, motorway, canal, railway, road. And just to complete the picture and get it all over and done with at one go, a helicopter buzzed around angrily. Everything was in a hurry, everything, it seemed, except the canal, twisting, twirling its way towards the ruins of Greenhalgh Castle and the market town of Garstang.

The castle comes into view a mile distant, a few stones standing together, the remains of a keep on a hillock, still resisting the wind and the rain after five hundred years. The castle had been built by Lord Derby in 1490 to protect surrounding lands. It stood for the King during the Civil War 150 years later, and it fell for the King when Oliver Cromwell's troops razed it – all except the jumble of stones, every one a different size and shape, all put together in walls five and six feet thick with so much skill it could be there another five hundred years. It did not seem to need the protection notice from the Department of the Environment warning about 'injury or defacement to this scheduled ancient monument'.

The castle stands eighty yards from a farm, and two hundred yards from the canal which snakes past it to the quaint old town of Garstang, through the parish of Barnacre-with-Bonds and across the great Wyre aqueduct, second only to the one over the Lune at Lancaster. Among the collection of bridges over the canal around Garstang are the remains of one that used to carry the Garstang, Pilling and Knott End Railway, long since gone. Ivy climbs the supports on the other side of the water; brambles and trees sprout from the towpath side. I climbed the banking to the top of the old bridge base and looked down the line from Garstang, across the Moss, past Scronkey and Little Tongues, almost off the end of Lancashire at Knott End-on-Sea. I looked and looked and saw nothing. Nothing but a huge, flat field that had covered the old line long ago.

'Bit fresh this morning,' a man called from the bridge carrying the road to Winmarleigh, a man on a bicycle, his raincoat flapping in the fresh breeze blowing from the Lune Estuary, shaping and slanting the trees. The canal slides on between Clifton Hill and Crookhey Hall, through Richmond Basin constructed for the shipping of stone from the now disused nearby quarry. The A6 is near at hand again, near enough to be heard as the canal goes through the Ellel Grange Estate and past the three-mile branch to Glasson Dock, past Galgate Wharf through to a cutting, two miles long, tree-lined and restful with picnic tables in spaces cut out of the embankment.

Once clear of the cutting, Lancaster starts to appear. The Ashton Memorial stands out to the right, and a road into the city joins the path as the canal moves out of the trees for a spectacular view of the castle and priory church standing together on the hill. The flag was flying and the sight was splendidly ancient. Close by are the roofless remains of the old packet boat house, built to hold two boats and with a hoist to lift boats to the upper floor for repairs.

For the first time in nearly thirty miles the towpath changes sides, and with it come the stables for the horses and Westmorland Brewery's Water Witch with a cobbled front and tables by the water. The A6 crosses here near the Farmer's Arms and the Alexandra Hotel, and as I walked along it towards the castle, I was somehow not surprised to see, in this still essentially country city, a shepherd with a sheep on a lead at the zebra crossing. The view from the graveyard of the fifteenth-century priory church next to the castle is stunning, across to Grange and Morecambe Bay, Furness Fells and the hills of southern Lakeland. I could not make out the canal from the castle, but I could see the castle from the canal as I passed near the town hall clock and Yates & Jackson's brewery before swinging left to cross the Lune by an aqueduct considered by many to be the high spot of a visit to the Lancaster Canal. For somebody brought up in a region teeming

St Mary's Gate, Lancaster, just below the castle.

with viaducts and aqueducts, some of them breathtaking, one more seemed hardly here or there. At least, so I thought until confronted with the view down river with the castle, a confusion of ridges, of ups and downs, and its church drawing the eye. Upstream are the M6 motorway and the Fells; beneath is a river a hundred yards wide, bridged by the magnificent John Rennie aqueduct.

As I approached Hest Bank, a Waterways Board boat appeared, pushing a barge carrying dredgings and low in the water, advancing like a hippopotamus, its nose just managing to stay above the surface. One good wave, I thought, and she's gone! One of the canal's familiar milestones, looking pretty in blue, had the number three on one side and twenty-four on the other. That was the old canal distances from Lancaster and Kendal. The land is not particularly flat, but of rolling hills. The castle was still in sight three miles to the rear, but it was soon to be replaced by the beauty of the Lakeland Hills, the Furness Fells, Grange across the water, and the coastline running away towards Barrow. It is a marvellous view across Morecambe Bay as the canal moves within a few hundred yards of the shore at Hest Bank. The green fields, the road, the grey of the shore and the glass of the water, the Peaks beyond, all making a memorable scene.

The view holds past Bolton-le-Sands with its Packet Boat Hotel, a reminder of the days between 1833 and 1846 when packet boats sailed the canal, doing the fifty-six mile round trip from Preston to Kendal in a day. There is not much of the navigable canal left as it goes through Carnforth and past Borwick Hall, visited by King Charles II, whose army camped in a nearby field. Boats can go only as far as Tewitfield, where the canal runs up against the embankment on which the road to Burton runs over the motorway and where the old Tewitfield locks, now right next to the M6 motorway, have been stepped and waterfalled.

The canal, though shallow and narrow in parts, keeps going for eight more miles, over the border into Cumbria past Holme and under the steep Farleton Fells, under the road to the Lakes and the motorway again before running out of water near Stainton. The canal is culverted at motorway and major road crossings, and at Field End, near Stainton, had been taken over for experiments by Liverpool University. Near Crooklands is a small stable capable of holding two horses. The door was open and there were

The village of Stainton where the Lancaster Canal
runs out of water, a few miles below Kendal.

holes in the roof, but the walls were sound. The troughs were still there, deep ones for food, shallow ones for water. A short, energetic man from a nearby garden left off picking his brussels sprouts. 'Last time the stables were used when commercial traffic was running would be in 1944, although we kept them going, bringing clay up from Preston by barge to seal the leaks in the canal bed. I put the last horse in that stable myself. I would think about 1950.'

The call of the Lakeland hills lured me on close to Kendal itself. The water finishes near the delightful village of Stainton, one of those places that nature holds dear and protects. The bed of the canal, however, can be traced on its remaining six or seven miles to Kendal, through open fields with bridges arching their backs over nothing. Even the Sedgwick aqueduct still stands, next to the village post office and with a bridge 9½ feet wide and capable of taking only one vehicle at a time. Thirty-six steps climb from the road to the canal bed, weed-ridden and filled in, but still there. Still clinging on to life after nearly two hundred years.

DISTANCE OF WALK: 42 MILES.   **OS MAPS 97 and 102**

23

Ripon Canal

There is not much to the Ripon Canal. Just 2¼ miles from the foot of the cathedral to the middle of the Ure, the river that runs through Wensleydale. But short though it is, the Ripon has a couple of notable points – the interesting town that gives it its name, and its position as the most northerly point in England that is connected to the waterways network. The Lancaster Canal goes further north but is cut off from the system.

Ripon, which lies just off the A1 in Yorkshire, is an exquisite little cathedral city with a population of under thirteen thousand. But it is the biggest town for a few miles around, a town of great charm, a polite town that has not got carried away with its own importance despite its position as a cathedral city. The cathedral itself dates from the twelfth century, although it does stand over a crypt that was part of the original building, constructed in the seventh century. It contains a narrow passage through which women of the time had to pass if their chastity was in doubt. The passage is known as Wilfrid's Needle, after the saint who developed the church, and if a woman could squeeze her way through, all was well.

One day I shall stay in Ripon until nine o'clock so I can witness a ceremony that goes back over a thousand years, the sounding of the horn at the market place. It was the duty of the wakeman – the watchman – to sound the watch, and if any house was robbed before sunrise and he was at fault – say having a snooze or a snorter somewhere – compensation had to be paid. It was an early form of insurance, with householders contributing a few pence a year as a tax and to cover the expenses of the watch. The sixteenth-century Wakeman's House stands at the corner of the market place, and they do say the building is haunted.

The canal, too, is fairly old, dating back to 1773, when it was part of a scheme to make the River Ure more navigable. The upper part of the canal was abandoned in 1955, leaving the bottom half fit for boats and still linked to the network.

A car-park attendant directed me to the canal. 'Across the west front of the Minster, down the hill, left at the roundabout and tha'll see where it starts.' I did – on the other side of the road to Boroughbridge (six miles) and York (twenty-three). I walked through the shells of buildings to see the sad ending of the canal, silted though still in water, up against the old warehouse and wharf manager's house. The canal runs with the Boroughbridge road for half a mile, overpowered by trees, brightened by big bunches of yellow iris, before turning right past the lovely Lock House and heading for the side of Littlethorpe. Ripon Angling Association uses the perfectly proper but pompous sounding word 'piscatorial' in its notice as the canal moves off into the country to regain some of its style. The Ripon Motor Boat Club basin, with about 150 boats moored, marks the limit of the navigable part of the canal. Ripon race-course is to the left, with the six-furlong straight marker close to the path. The grass on the towpath was being cut. 'You can go right down to Roecliffe by the side of the water,' I was told. 'Cross this bridge, go past Newby Hall, cross the field that brings you out at the church at Roecliffe.'

Poppies and tall, handsome, purple thistles stood at the side of the canal which runs into the Ure at Oxclose Lock after a pleasant fifty-minute stroll. The river is about sixty yards wide, and in the distance, downstream, I could make out Newby Hall among the trees. A small sign bearing a yellow arrow and the words 'Yoredale Way' took me along the riverside, through gates and thigh-high grass. 'Yore' was the original word for 'Ure', and the district was commonly known as Yoredale before taking its present name from the small town of Wensley near the foot of the dale. The old name persists, however, with such as Burton-on-Yore and Clifton-on-Yore. The river sweeps lazily past Newby Hall, a splendid Queen Anne mansion with fine statues and tapestries and gardens noted for flowering shrubs and rock gardens. The path becomes a road, emerging at an open army encampment where tables had·been laid for dinner in the marquees. The bottles of wine were a great temptation to a passing traveller, weary of foot and suffering from that terrible disease, drought of the throat.

I kept with the river, searching for a path that was becoming obscure and finding the little yellow arrow tucked away on a metal gate. After passing Westwick Lock, the path deteriorates, entering a wood, becoming extremely muddy in parts and, not

The 1875 school building at Roecliffe.

surprisingly, eventually vanishing. Yellow iris are everywhere, the grass and weeds continue at waist height and, after striking up through the wood, I followed the fence and barbed wire to the water's edge to find the arrow. The going had become tough but still manageable. A waist-high aisle of poppies at the edge of a wheat field, all blowing gently in the breeze, is followed by head-high thistles and more grass and wheat and poppies.

The great variety of wild life is one of the joys of canal and riverside walking. I almost fell over a partridge at the edge of the wheat field, and I do not know which of us was the more startled as I recoiled and she whirred away towards the trees, leaving her three little ones to wander into the wheat. I moved away quickly so mother and children would not become too far apart, and followed a fence uphill to Roecliffe church and another yellow Yoredale arrow. I sat for a few minutes near the 1875 school building of Roecliffe before walking the mile and a half to Boroughbridge, once an important coaching station on the Great North Road with one of the route's greatest hostelries, the Crown, with stables for a hundred horses. As I neared the town, I passed the site of the Devil's Arrows, three huge megalithic stones standing in a field, said to have been fired by the Devil about three thousand years ago. I preferred the little yellow arrows myself.

DISTANCE OF WALK: 2¼ MILES.   **OS MAP 99**

24

Pocklington Canal

The warmth of the bar-room at the Cross Keys in Melbourne was particularly welcoming after the crisp, cold air of the Pocklington Canal and the East Yorkshire Wolds. The solitude of the canal bank was matched by the emptiness of the pub, and the landlord had time enough to talk about a canal – 'nine miles and nine locks, you know' – involved in a lengthy restoration after years of neglect. 'They must have been at it fifteen years,' he mused. 'Keep doing bits, then stopping. Shortage of money.' I asked if it was worthwhile. 'Well, it's a pretty little canal,' he said with some fondness.

A pretty little canal. That it is, and as I strolled its lonely banks I knew he had to be right. Any preservation of heritage is worthwhile, but even more so when it adds to so many people's enjoyment in so many different ways. It might have taken some years, but now the Pocklington Canal is open to the world. At least, the bottom half of it is. Now boats can sail from around Church Bridge at Thornton into the Derwent, Ouse and Humber, past Bubwith, Barmby on the Marsh and Boothferry, and out into the big world. This is the land of open spaces, of becks and plantations, of Wolds and Forestry Commission, where Pocklington, with its four thousand population and its notable school, is the biggest place for miles. The canal was one of the latest in the country to be built, completed in 1818 and running from the Derwent to a mile below Pocklington. It was not taken any closer to the town because of cost and water shortage and finished up smack against the road from Hull to York, taking the produce of the country away, bringing raw materials back. The canal's thriving time was not long. Neglect set in, and by 1905 receipts were down to £49. The last keel skipper sold out and bought a lorry in 1932, and at Easter two years later the last pleasure traffic sailed up to Melbourne.

It was a raw November morning when I left the car at Hagg Bridge and walked the mile or two to East Cottingwith through fields still deathly white from the overnight frost. My breath joined the morning air like puffs of smoke from a power station's cooling tower. But what do they know of power stations, the people of Menagerie Farm, Cheescatie and Sheepwalk Farms, where the only disturbance across the face of the Wold comes, as it always has done, from the towers and spires of ancient churches?

A sign at the entrance to the canal from the placid waters of the Derwent, once tidal, now freshwater, points the way for all craft into the Pocklington Canal and proclaims: 'Wheldrake Ings Nature Reserve. Quiet please.' I tiptoed through the grass and winced as it crunched deafeningly beneath my feet. A few cows grazed across the river, the familiar picture of English peace. The only sound was the dull rumble of a lorry in the distant whiteness. Then quiet. Until a great gaggle of geese from the nature reserve noisily patrolled the area, vigorously flapping their wings as if trying to get warm. The canal was frozen on the surface but nothing serious enough to stop a pair of swans from breaking through. There is a saying among farmers in Hampshire that if the ice bears a duck in November, it will not do so again through the winter. We were not far away from it that morning.

Strictly speaking, I suppose, the Pocklington Canal goes through nowhere. It starts near East Cottingwith, brushes Melbourne and Bielby and falls short of Pocklington. On a misty morning you could miss all of them and see nothing but fields and farms and trees, cattle and sheep, swedes and cabbages. This was almost such a morning.

Through the haze I could just make out the handful of buildings that make up East Cottingwith. A path and a lane took me among them, past farms and the Blue Bell Inn to the small, towered Georgian church of St Mary's in so isolated a part of England that the visitors' book, fittingly started by the Bishop, Bernard Hey Wood, in 1930, has still used fewer than thirty pages. A notice near the door, dated from the middle of last century, tells of the number of 'free seats' in the church having been increased by sixty-seven:

'The accommodation in this chapel was increased by rearranging the seats in the year 1846 by which means additional accommodation for 26 persons was obtained. A grant of £25 in aid of the undertaking was made by the Incorporated Society for Promoting the Enlargement, Building and Repairing of churches and chapels on condition that one hundred and twenty two seats described in the annexed plan should be set apart and declared to be free and unappropriated for ever. The provision of church room previously to the alteration being to the extent of 176 seats, 55 of which number were free.'

Among the gravestones surrounding the church is one with an engraving of a duck in flight: 'To the memory of Snowden Slights. Wildfowler of East Cottingwith. Born June 14 1829. Died April 15 1913.' But it is the inscription on the wall of the church near the gate that really took my fancy, engraved by a man not only to the memory of his recently departed wife but also to himself, when his time should arrive. It is dated 1762.

'To the memory of Ann the wife of Robert Gray who died November 1761 aged 86. Also in memory of the above said Robert Gray when he departs this life in hopes of a happy resurrection whenever one must give account to God how with life they lived. All those that comes to our gravestone as we are now so must you be. Repent therefore without delay. You little know your dying day. Then live so here that when you die your soul may rest with God and Christ on high. Engraved by Robert Gray.' The date 1762 is followed underneath by 1775, probably the year he died. You little know your dying day . . .

It was high time to move on, down the lane past the cemetery, back to the canal where half a dozen boats were moored. The towpath quickly changes sides at Storwood to run on a piece of land about thirty feet wide between two waters, the canal and the Beck, which also heads for the Derwent. Before I was back at Hagg Bridge, I had seen a heron, kingfisher and pheasant and two more pairs of swans, cutting their way through the thinning ice, getting a closer look at the stranger who was disturbing their morning. Just beyond the bridge comes Gardham Lock, with a swing bridge and a notice warning 'Private Shooting'. The path around here is almost as wide as the field itself, and sheep, unlike the swans, shied away out of the range of the intruder.

The canal slides along the bottom of the village of Melbourne, which straggles along the road from Sutton upon Derwent to Pocklington. Its curious little Victorian church of St Monica, set back from the main road, is in grey and red, its walls of corrugated iron on the outside and boarded on the inside. There was little life in the village that lunchtime, a quiet stretch of a place with its empty pub. The landlord told me about the arm of the canal which extended to behind 'The Cross Keys' to what was a coal wharf. And of the bridge over the canal until somebody tried to go over it in a tractor. The timber deck collapsed into the water but the driver was able to escape without too much trouble. Many local residents used it to get on to the towpath for a stroll; others claimed a right of way to their land on the other side. I crossed over on a home-made footbridge, a tree sliced down the middle like a banana with a hand-rail and a warning: 'Cross at own risk.'

Seven of the nine locks are in the last half of the canal, and I stood for a time staring into one, its gate broken and holey, the iron balance wheel at an unlikely angle, a reminder that it has not been used for fifty years. The path is through flat, open land with the tree-lined Bielby Arm branching off and men in nearby fields lopping swedes and attending to cabbages. The path narrows with the arrival of a hawthorn hedge where wild roses and brambles grow; more derelict locks are passed, and weeds gather as Canal Head approaches. I was interested to read later the log of Capt. J. Carr-Ellison's waterway exploration aboard *Thetis* in the early 1930s. 'Arrived off the junction with the Pocklington Canal at 12.45. Got up the cut leading to the lock at East Cottingwith but found on our arrival there that the canal above the lock was covered with weed. Went ashore and walked some distance up only to find that the canal itself was entirely overgrown so that one could almost walk across. Agreed the conditions were impossible.' Slowly, through the devotion of the Pocklington Canal Amenity Society, the canal is returning to normal. Canal Head itself is a picture, a pleasant picnic area with a sign announcing the Towing Path Walk with Melbourne five miles and East Cottingwith 9¾. The lock cottage and the warehouse have been restored, seats have been provided, and yes, restoration is worthwhile for one of the country's prettiest little canals.

DISTANCE OF WALK: 9¾ MILES.   **OS MAP 106**

25

Chesterfield Canal

There is a charm about Chesterfield, a warmth that somehow stems from the corkscrew spire of its parish church. It gives the place an air of eccentricity; it is like something straight out of a nursery rhyme. Whenever I go, I know I would not be surprised to find a crooked man and a crooked stile and any number of crooked sixpences just around the corner. I know it only has something to do with the wood and lead that were used in building the spire, the sun at work on the green, unseasoned wood and softening the lead. But I live in hope that one day I will hear a marvellous, colourful legend about it instead.

The spire has been that way for rather a long time. The Reverend MacRitchie, went through in 1795, on the way from Sharrow to London. The reverend gentleman was apparently wide awake despite having set out at half past 3 a.m., 'with Mr McKenzie's boy carrying my saddle-bags to the Tollbar separating the counties of York and Derby, where take my seat on the stage-coach at half-past four. Breakfast at Chesterfield, remarkable for its twisted spire, apparently crooked, and like to fall.'

Mr MacRitchie probably foretold the weather, too. For the spire still leans tipsily over the town like a happy drunk. And as far as I could see, the locals do not spend too much time looking over their shoulders, anxious to see if this is the day the spire is at last going to fall over in a dizzy stupor. It got used to its deformity long ago and will continue to gaze down for a year or two yet, I reckon, on the old town with its alleys and cobbles, on its Knifesmithgate and Saltergate, the Shambles and the Market Place and the Royal Oak, and Holy Trinity Church where George Stephenson was buried in the chancel in 1848.

Not that Chesterfield has all that much to do with the Chesterfield Canal now. Those days are long gone, a roof collapse on the long and troublesome Norwood Tunnel cutting the canal in two with the top part, about ten miles to Chesterfield, being left stranded. This waterway was among the early ones, opening in 1777 and running forty-six miles from Chesterfield through Worksop and East Retford to the River Trent at West Stockwith, and providing a better outlet through Nottinghamshire to the Humber for the products of North Derbyshire and South Yorkshire. Before that, the goods went by pack mule to Bawtry, then by boat. Coal, of course, became the canal's main carrying commodity but other cargoes included stone, corn, lime, lead, timber, iron, pottery and ale. The last commercial traffic was from the brickyards at Walkeringham to West Stockwith in 1955. Not bad, 178 years of cargo-carrying, with the most notable probably coming in 1840 with the start of 250,000 tons of Anston stone bound for London and the new Houses of Parliament.

Goods were transferred to larger vessels at West Stockwith, a remote village close up against the Trent on the Nottinghamshire border. But with its nearest bridges five miles to the south and twelve miles to the north, West Stockwith might as well be at the sea. Even its next-door neighbour, East Stockwith, just across the river, is ten miles away by road.

I went to West Stockwith from Gainsborough. I could have walked the five miles on the banks of the Trent. I probably would have had to if a bus had not been ready to go. 'Stockwith?' queried the driver. 'East or West? Makes quite a difference.' I got off close to the basin, bristling with boats of all shapes and undergoing some hefty-looking repairs which had closed one of the locks into the Trent. The mist hung heavily all about, damp and clinging, just the sort of weather that should have sent the Romans, the Vikings, the Normans scurrying home in despair and leaving this country to the pure Brits. If ever there has been such a thing. I strolled around and stuck my nose up against the windows of one or two buildings and boats before looking across the river to East Stockwith with its clutch of houses and tiny, steepled church within a stone's throw.

It must have been the mist, or perhaps the isolation was having some effect, but the water in the canal had a greeny, turquoisy, Mediterranean look. The two chimneys sticking their noses high in the air on the right just had to be England though. Within a few minutes I was at the Packet Inn, near Misterton, named after the packet boats which ran fifteen miles to Retford from the outlying villages on market days. The canal cut round the bottom of the

The basin at West Stockwith, the start of
the Chesterfield Canal.

village, under Wharf Road where a willow tree wept into the water and a footbridge accompanied the narrow road overhead. 'Is it going to clear up?' an angler asked through the mist. I shrugged and pressed on through the fields, one teeming with turnips, another newly ploughed, one still rough with wheat stubble. The canal left Walkeringham a mile to the left but passed the brick yard which had carried the village name.

A man in overalls watched me from the bridge, wished me a 'Mornin'', then followed to see me emerge from the other side. 'This is t' brick works, you know,' he called. 'Well, used to be. Must have closed up, let's see, twenty-five year ago. There used to be narrow boats wi' horses, tekkin' bricks to t' Trent. And they used to bring coal here from Shireoaks.' He pronounced Shireoaks almost the way I would say Shorrocks. 'But it's all changed. Little man can't stand up to t' big uns, you know.'

The land is flat, more Lincolnshire than Nottinghamshire, with little to be seen but fields. Fields and hedges, hedges and fields. A couple of telephone wires were hanging about as if spun by a spider, one running to Leys Farm where hundreds of rolled-up bales of hay were stacked outside. Soon I was able to make out the shapes of houses and chimneys, blurred by the mist, up on the hill. Gringley on the Hill. I saw, too, what looked to be the base of a windmill.

After Gringley Lock the canal turned into a bed of leaves from the trees on the bank. Ash, lime, sycamore, reds and browns and yellows, a hundred hues to make the prettiest patchwork quilt. Two sharp left turns at Cuckoo Hill send the canal on an about-face, one of them taking it through the short Drakeholes Tunnel, the path going over the hill and past a two-hundred-year-old pub, once, it seems, called the White Swan, now the Griff Inn. The canal then skirts Wiseton Hall, a beautiful piece of country where the colours of the leaves seemed to be even deeper and stronger. The village of Wiseton makes a pleasing picture over the hedge, with farm buildings and crisp, clean houses topped by tall chimneys. The peace was broken but not destroyed by the clock clanging out the hour.

The road to Clayworth forms the path for a few hundred yards, and once back in the country the pheasants were soon evident, scuttering or whirring away to a safer part of the field where they could continue their hunt for grain or seed in peace. The canal avoids Clayworth like a by-pass road, and it was along here I came across the first milepost, with the number 37. That had to be the number of miles to Chesterfield. Here are the moorings for the Retford and Worksop Boat Club, with a smithy and canalside houses making a beautiful launching pad for a run of about two miles, without a bridge, to Hayton with its church. There is a plaque on the tower: 'Sacred to the memory of the Rev. John Mason late vicar of Hayton cum Tylne upwards of 11 years and formerly vicar of Skipsea in Yorkshire, died 22 December 1844 aged 70 years.'

The canal continues through this flat land of wide open spaces towards its first lock for nine miles. I doubt if there can be a more intriguing, thought-provoking title for a lock anywhere in England: Whitsunday Pie Lock! It was given this wonderful name after a local farmer's wife had produced a large pie to celebrate completion of the lock on Whitsunday. I was disappointed to see that the Chesterfield Canal Society, in their own production on the canal, say the lock was 'supposedly so-called' because of the story of the completion. Lovely, legendary stories like these should be preserved as fact not supposition. I have no doubts at all that the farmer's wife did indeed produce a huge pie for the workers. God bless her.

The lock marks the run-in to Retford, split into East and West by the River Idle and once a fairly important stopping place on the old Great North Road. The noble tower of St Swithin's reigns over the large market square where the White Heart is the only remaining old posting house, one of the most important before Retford was by-passed by the A1. The canal has a surprisingly pleasant run through the town. I noticed road signs for Newark and Lincoln as I walked along behind the fire station, an old 'furniture repository' with doors that opened on to the water, and the high school where the girls were having a quick smoke by the canal. On through attractive parkland, past 'Protestant Place 1826', and out of the town between lines of trees, their leaves beautifully colour-splashed.

The canal is soon back in its more familar surroundings, rural and level with the occasional low, narrow bridge. The Forest Locks, once the Sherwood Forest Locks, appear out of nowhere, and over to the right I could make out the traffic on the road between Retford and Blyth. Just before the last of the Forest Locks

Chesterfield Canal at East Retford.

the canal crosses a straight road once used by the Romans and which was the original coaching road before the citizens of Retford managed to get it diverted through their town. The ploughed fields were a picture of neatness; the farmers were hard at work in one of the busiest, most important periods of the year on the land.

The canal is approaching the throbbing motor life of the A1 highway and runs alongside it for about a mile before crossing it at Ranby and heading directly for Worksop nearly five miles away. The gloom of dusk was beginning to settle, car lights were being switched on as the canal and the main road from Retford stayed reasonably close together on the way into Worksop. Dusk was gathering and hid many of the delights of the stretch through Osberton Hall Park, a beautifully maintained country estate. But nothing could hide the lovely stables, close to the canal, with their clock tower. The River Ryton also ran alongside as I headed into Worksop, guided by the lights of the town and comforted by the glow and rattle of Manton Colliery on the outskirts.

It is no longer possible to get beyond Worksop by boat, although lengths of the canal are in water, including the Summit pound where Chesterfield Canal Society have their trip boat, the *Norwood Packet*. But much has been lost, swallowed by industry and housing, a great shame for a lovely canal.

DISTANCE OF WALK: 26 MILES.   **OS MAP 112 and 120**

Lincoln Cathedral, in view for 20 miles on
the Fossdyke and Witham Navigations.

26

Fossdyke and Witham Navigations

My lasting impression of one of England's oldest stretches of navigable water is the overpowering presence of the cathedral at Lincoln. For about seven hours, for something approaching twenty miles, the beautiful church is in sight, at first just a scratch on the horizon drawing the traveller ever on, and finally revealed in glorious detail. I first spotted it at Saxilby, a sprawl of a town on the Fossdyke, and felt the flush of excitement the pilgrims must have experienced hundreds of years ago. And as the day wore wearily on and the loneliness of the Lincolnshire Fenlands washed over me, I turned to it for the comfort of familiarity.

The loneliness is almost unbearable at times. No other waterway provides so much solitude for such long periods. For miles there is no sign of a towpath, and the only reminders of life are the cries of the birds, disturbed and distressed by the tramp of boots through the overgrowth. Herons, with their sharp eye for the unfamiliar sign of life on the landscape, rise a hundred yards away, unhurried, forewarned, rising lazily into the sky, whirling, dropping two hundred yards behind. Partridges show no such elegance or awareness. They doze on in their balls of grass, tucked away out of the wind, oblivious to the danger of an intruder. The clump of boots is on their doorstep before they fly off, startled, squawking like frightened children, their wings flapping desperately fast as they get the hell out of it. The only thing the two birds have in common is their ability to fly. One watchful and alert, never caught unawares, like a well-organized hostess; the other half asleep, always at the last minute, the perfect prey for the poacher. Dozy old thing.

I walked miles and saw nobody. Flat patchwork fields stretch in every direction, their spread interrupted only occasionally by the bump of a farmhouse, a cluster of trees thrown together like farmers gossiping at the market. Those who say this land is crowded ought to take another look. And as the North Sea approaches, the wind freshens, the face tingles with the sharpness and bite of a wind reaching its peak. In its quiet stretches the Fossdyke and Witham still belongs to the Romans who widened and straightened the River Witham and cut out the connecting Fossdyke. In nearly two thousand years little can have changed. More straightening, some deepening, but it is still easy to see the Romans sailing to Lincoln, the Danes nosing their way to more looting and rioting, the Normans transporting the stone for that wonderful cathedral.

It was early morning when I approached Torksey Lock, where the Fossdyke meets the Trent. The ruins of Torksey Castle, a mansion built in Elizabethan times, burnt by the Royalists during the Civil War, stands close by in a field of cows. But it was the towpath I wanted, not the castle. A boy, huddled, hurrying to school, looked in disbelief but pointed me in the right direction. Behind me, in the space of ten miles, were three power stations, their enormous egg-timers of chimneys pouring out white smoke, flattened by the wind, soon lost among the clouds scudding overhead.

I put my back to the power stations and got on to the high, grassy bank above the river. Lincoln was eleven miles away but already I was searching the horizon for its cathedral. Several pleasure boats had gathered at Torksey, and standing among them, large and menacing like the school bully who had pushed his way into the dinner queue, was a tub of a barge, maybe one of those Dutch barges I had heard about. I strode off towards the sun, watery and uncertain in the cloud-filled sky. Birds twittered in the hedge with all the early-morning excitement of a bunch of young office girls, the gorse nodded as I passed, pylons, one of man's more monstrous creations, trod the fields around.

The going was not easy. I began to realize why the huddler had hesitated when I asked for the towpath. It did not exist. The grass was high and wet from weeks of almost incessant rain, and it did not take long for the water to find its way into my boots. Soon I was wet from the knees down, and I felt like a plant left to stand in a bowl of water. Gradually the water was working its way up. I could only hope that my top half, soaking up the sun and the freshening breeze, could hold back the creeping tide of rising damp.

Far ahead I could see a road running alongside the water. A sign proclaimed: 'Fossdyke Navigation'; another pointed the way to 'Lincoln 8 (Skegness 51)'. At least now I was on the road, the A57 from Worksop to Lincoln – and presumably on to Skegness – and ignoring the bank and the water. After about an hour and a half's walking I was in Saxilby, exchanging 'Mornings' with the milkman, nodding cheerfully at a gnome and frog in a garden and peering enviously through the windscreen as the men from Telecom sucked into one of their morning brews. Here I got my first exciting glimpse of Lincoln Cathedral, high and commanding, beckoning me on. First I had to go with the water alongside the main street of Saxilby, a fairly deserted spot with the cherry blossom in full bloom, a chip shop, a 1907 Lincoln Co-op shop, two pubs, the inevitable Ship and the Sun, its face peeling rather nastily, a mounting block at its side. It was around these parts that a Roman silver statuette of Mars, now in the British Museum, was found on the bed of the river.

Once out of the village, the cathedral looms large and inviting. All around is flat, pleasant country, except dead ahead where the cathedral rises from the hill, standing high over the fields and meadows and budding trees, bursting to get into summer. A long, straight stretch of about three miles of water runs from Fiddler's Elbow – just about where the road and canal part – to Lincoln, a quiet, peaceful lane of water. A rabbit scuttled away startled; a trainload of industrial sand on the accompanying railway line shattered the peace. The line and the navigation are so close that the railway signals could well be for the boats as the cathedral comes closer and closer. The roofs of houses clustered around the feet of the cathedral are much clearer, the lines of the church more definite. My reverential reverie was rudely ended. 'Welcome to the Pyewipe, How nice. The Pyewipe, of course, turned out to be an inn, right on the river bank. Just a little early for me, thank you. I marched on, past the golf course and race-course with its magnificent pavilion, past dear old *Annie Barraclough*, standing high in the water, itching to sail off into other waters.

A low bridge heralds the entrance to the Port. 'Sound your horn.' *Sobriety*, a rather nice, squat, chunky barge, twin-funnelled, nosed up to the bridge, hooting impatiently before somebody came along after nearly ten minutes to raise the bridge. I was in the Port, Brayford Pool, apparently once so picturesque that artists almost jostled for position at its side. There are plenty

High Bridge, known also as the Glory Hole,
supports this 16th-century half-timbered house on
the Fossdyke and Witham Navigations in Lincoln.

of handsome boats and a wine barge, and the cathedral looks down lovingly as the Fossdyke turns into the Witham and leaves at the top left-hand corner. Out of the Pool, under the bridge and up to the Glory Hole, a bridge on which stands a black-and-white sixteenth-century building. There is a jeweller's and a café – 'Luncheon being served' – and the city was bustling with life as people spilled about, shopping, sightseeing, hunting for food. In the space of fifty yards I must have passed more people alongside the river than I had seen in the previous eleven miles.

But soon the city was behind me. The towpath became over-grown and unwalkable, and I had to take to a disused railway line on the other side of the hedge and alongside one of the numerous drains in Lincolnshire. Soon I was able to return to the path, ready to pass Washingborough village with its church tower and old railway station-master's house. The path quickly degener-ated again, becoming boggy and impossible, forcing me to the railway line where I trod the sleepers between the rusting rails.

Concentrating on treading the sleepers and avoiding the sharp stones between did not allow me to take in the scenery, and Cherry Willingham, partly obscured by soil whipped up by the wind, came and went quickly on the other side of the water. Another church tower, this time at Fiskerton, flitted into my vision before I reached Five Mile Bridge – that far from Lincoln – where a car ferry used to operate. I wish I had been able to visit the small Norman church at Fiskerton where, so I had read, a register dates back to 1559, with an item for 1806 which reads: 'Driest summer for 20 years. No rain from April Fair to 26th June. Conduit water taken from Lincoln to Boston . . . packet went to Boston by the drain. Praying for rain.' At Bardney Lock I turned round for the umpteenth time for the comfort of the cathedral, still gloriously commanding. Several iron barges stand on the opposite bank at Southrey, rusty, as much a part of the past as the old car ferry looking as if it had been left to rot at the water's edge. One of those odd-looking triangular planes flashed by, like those we used to make out of paper to whizz round the classroom.

The water winds gently through the fenlands, past the banked-up entrance to the old, disused canal that ran to Horncastle ten miles away. Tattershall Castle, apparently, is well worth seeing but it is a mile from the navigation, much, much too far when you have been walking all day.

This is the heart of the fen country, rich black soil, fertile and rewarding, and soon the welcome sight of the Boston Stump shows up, a 272-foot finger of the fourteenth-century St Botolph's Church pointing to the sky. Boston has been a seaport for more than eight hundred years, an attractive town littered with medieval architecture. Ten years after the *Mayflower* took the Pilgrim Fathers to America, another band of Puritans left Boston, so many of them coming from the town that they gave the name to the capital of Massachusetts. I was two months too early for the 4 July celebrations when the bond between Boston and the United States is displayed. A pity.

They do say that from the top of Boston Stump one third of the county can be seen, including Lincoln and much of the navigation. I did not bother going up. I had seen enough of it for one day. Anyway, my legs would not have been too thrilled.

DISTANCE OF WALK: 43 MILES   **OS MAPS 121, 122 and 131**

Index